JUST FOR FUN

By Debbie Mumm®

Have some quilting fun with this great gathering of projects. Play with color, add dimension, incorporate embroidery, try new techniques, or just enjoy lots of easy piecing with twenty-four fun projects. You'll find lots of inspiration for quilts and decorating accessories for everyone and everywhere … JUST FOR FUN!

Created for Leisure Arts by Debbie Mumm®

©2005 by Debbie Mumm
Leisure Arts, Inc., 5701 Ranch Drive, Little Rock, AR 72223
www.leisurearts.com

Dear Friends,

After nearly 20 years of quilt designs and 50 books, I still had quilt ideas rolling around in my head with no place to go! So, we put many of them together in this book…just for fun! Big quilts, sweet quilts, masculine quilts, whimsical quilts all found a home in this book. From playing with color to embroidering ants to painting polka dot borders, you'll find lots of fun new techniques. With this unique and varied assortment of projects, I think you'll find a quilt for everyone and everywhere.

We had fun composing with color in the Color Spectrum Quilt and Sorbet Lap Quilt. A sense of movement was the goal for the gorgeous Spindrift Quilt. A fun setting for a sampler quilt creates blocks within blocks for the Around the Block Quilt. A variety of dimensional flowers poke out of purses in Pocketbook Full of Posies Wall Quilt. Embroidery highlights our Friendship Flowers Wall Quilt and the Guardian Angel Crib Quilt. Scottie dogs deck the corners of the Argyle Quilt and luscious limes bring colorful energy to a floor cloth and wall quilt. Hit the beach with our Playful Picnic Quilt or Summer Sun Beach Throw or hit the road with our luggage-themed wall quilt. If you have a passion for shoes, (like I do!) kick up your heels with a fun shoe wallhanging or enjoy butterflies and bees on a uniquely finished wall quilt. You're sure to have as much fun making these quilts as I had designing them!

Get yourself a cup of passion fruit tea, put on your favorite slippers and spend a few minutes of delight as you browse for ideas and inspiration in this new book filled with fun and fantastic quilt projects. You're sure to have a hard time deciding which project to do first!

Get out your fabric stash, rev up your machine, and start sewing…just for fun!

Enjoy!

Debbie Mumm

Table of Contents

POCKETBOOK FULL OF POSIES

41½" x 41½" • Wall Quilt

Delightful sprays of pert posies peek from the tops of the handbags in this darling wall quilt. "Real" pockets and a variety of 3-D flora–along with embellishments such as couching, buttons, and cording–add dimension and whimsy to the simply-pieced blocks.

FABRIC REQUIREMENTS & CUTTING INSTRUCTIONS

Read all instructions before beginning and use ¼"-wide seam allowances throughout. Read Cutting Strips and Pieces on page 108 prior to cutting fabrics.

Pocketbook Full of Posies Wall Quilt 41½" x 41½"	FIRST CUT		SECOND CUT	
	Number of Strips or Pieces	Dimensions	Number of Pieces	Dimensions
Fabric A *Purse Backgrounds* ⅝ yard *(Star Flower & Primrose Blocks & Star Flower Backing)* ⅜ yard *(Bell Flower & Marigold Blocks)*	1* 2* 1*	6½" x 42" 2" x 42" 1½" x 42" *Cut for each fabric	2* 2* 8* 4*	6½" x 14½" 2" x 14½" 2" squares 1½" x 7"
Fabric B *Purse* ¼ yard each of four fabrics	1*	5½" x 12½" *Cut for each fabric		
Fabric C *Purse Trim* ⅛ yard each of three fabrics	1*	2" x 12½" *Cut one each for two fabrics & two of one fabric		
Fabric D *Purse Pockets* Assorted Scraps	2 2 2 1 1 2 1 2	5" x 11" (Star Flower Striped Pocket) 3" x 7" (Marigold Blue Pocket) 3" x 5" (Marigold Gold Pocket Flap) 3" x 5" (Marigold Blue Pocket Flap) 6" x 8" (Primrose Tan Pocket) 5¾" x 4¾" (Primrose Green Pocket) 5½" x 4⅝" (Primrose Checked Pocket) 3" x 6" (Primrose Green Pocket Flap)		
Fabric E *Block Accent Border* ⅓ yard	8	1" x 42"	8 8	1" x 15½" 1" x 14½"
Fabric F *Sashing* ½ yard	6	2" x 42"	2 3 2	2" x 35" 2" x 32" 2" x 15½"
BORDERS				
Outside Border ½ yard	4	3½" x 42"		
Binding ½ yard	5	2¾" x 42"		

Pocketbook Full of Posies Wall Quilt continued
Backing - 2⅝ yard
Batting - 46" x 46" & Scraps
Marigold Purse Trim Appliqué - 1½" x 9½" scrap
Dimensional Flower Appliqués -
Star Flower - ⅙ yard blue fabric
Bell Flower - ⅛ yard yellow fabric
Marigold Flower - ¼ yard gold fabric
Primrose Flower - ⅙ yard red fabric
Appliqué Leaves & Stems - ⅛ yard each of four fabrics
Bell Flowers Stem & Leaves - ¼ yard of each
Star Flower Purse Handle - 3½" x 14" bias strip
Primrose Purse Handle Appliqué - Scrap
Yarn & Silk Ribbon (stems) - ½ yard of each
Decorative Cording & Braid (handles) - ⅓ yard each
⅜" Cotton Filler Cord - ⅓ yard
Green Embroidery Floss
Template Plastic or Cardboard
Lightweight Fusible Web - 1 yard
Six Assorted Buttons
Five Assorted Yellow Beads

GETTING STARTED

This quilt includes four 15½" square (unfinished) blocks: Star Flower Purse (top left), Bell Flower Purse (top right), Marigold Purse (bottom left), and Primrose Purse (bottom right). The basic purse blocks are constructed in exactly the same fashion—just the fabrics are different–but that's where the similarities end as each is embellished with its own unique detail and dimensional flowers and leaves.

Since quilting with dimensional elements can be a challenge, this quilt is assembled and quilted prior to adding the flower elements. Make templates for all patterns on pages 11-12 from plastic or cardboard.

Refer to Accurate Seam Allowance on page 108. Whenever possible, use the Assembly Line Method on page 108. Press seams in direction of arrows.

PURSE BLOCKS

1. Sew one 2" x 12½" Fabric C strip to one 5½" x 12½" Fabric B strip as shown. Press. Referring to photo on page 4, make four, one of each color combination.

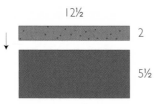

12½

2

5½

Make 4
(one of each color combination)

2. Refer to Quick Corner Triangles on page 108. Sew four 2" Fabric A squares to each unit from step 1 as shown matching background fabrics. Press. Make four, one of each color combination.

Fabric A = 2" x 2"
Unit from step 1
Make 4
(one of each color combination)

3. Sew each unit from step 2 between two matching 1½" x 7" Fabric A pieces as shown. Press. Make four, one of each color combination.

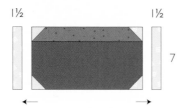

1½   1½

7

Make 4
(one of each color combination)

4. Refer to layout on page 10 for position of units from step 3. Sew each unit from step 3 between one matching 6½" x 14½" Fabric A strip and one 2" x 14½" Fabric A strip as shown. Press. Make four, one of each color combination.

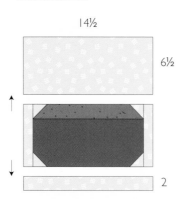

14½

6½

2

Make 2
(one of each color combination)

14½

6½

2

Make 2
(one of each color combination)

5. Sew each unit from step 4 between two 1" x 14½" Fabric E strips as shown. Press. Sew 1" x 15½" Fabric E strips to sides. Press. Make four, one of each color combination.

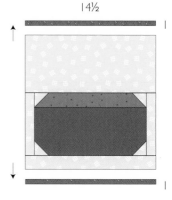

14½   1

1

Make 4
(one of each color combination)

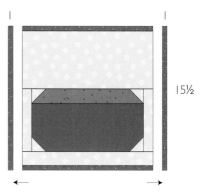

1   1

15½

Make 4
(one of each color combination)

ASSEMBLY

1. Refer to photo on page 4 and quilt layout on page 10. Sew one 2" x 15½" Fabric F strip between two blocks. Press seams toward Fabric F. Make two rows.

2. Referring to layout on page 10, arrange and sew three 2" x 32" Fabric F strips and rows from step 1. Press seams toward Fabric F.

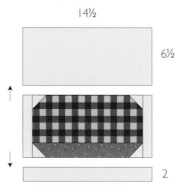

3. Sew 2" x 35" Fabric F strips to sides of unit from step 2. Press.

4. Measure quilt through center from side to side. Cut two 3½"-wide Outside Border strips to that measurement. Sew to top and bottom of quilt. Press seams toward border.

5. Measure quilt through center from top to bottom, including borders just added. Cut two 3½"-wide Outside Border strips to that measurement. Sew to sides of quilt. Press.

ADDING THE POCKETS

1. For Star Flower Block place two 5" x 11" Fabric D pieces right sides together. Using ¼"-wide seam, sew around edges, leaving a 3" opening for turning. Clip corners, turn, and press. Hand-stitch opening closed.

2. Using a temporary fabric marker, mark pocket front as shown. Fold 2¼" marked lines on top of 1" marked lines to form pleats. Press. From bottom edge of pocket, edge-stitch halfway up along folds and anchor stitching. Referring to photo on page 4 and block layout on page 8, position and edge-stitch pocket to Star Flower purse along pocket sides and bottom edge.

| 10½
| 2¼ | 2¼ |

3. For Marigold Block, trace Marigold Large Flap template (page 11) on one 3" x 5" Fabric D (gold) piece. Place marked fabric and matching 3" x 5" Fabric D piece right sides together over batting scrap. Stitch on drawn line, leaving top edge free of stitches. Cut out flap, trimming batting close to stitching and leaving ³⁄₁₆"-wide seam allowance. Clip curves, turn right side out. Press.

4. Refer to Quick-Fuse Appliqué on page 109. Trace Small Flap template on fusible web and fuse to wrong side of contrasting 3" x 5" Fabric D (blue) piece. Fuse Small Flap to Large Flap from step 3. Finish appliqué edges with machine satin stitch or decorative stitching as desired.

5. Using Marigold Purse Pocket template (page 12), trace template on wrong side of one 3" x 7" Fabric D piece. Place marked fabric and matching 3" x 7" Fabric D piece right sides together over batting scrap. Stitch on drawn line, leaving a 3" opening for turning. Cut out pocket, trim batting close to stitching, and trim seam allowance to ³⁄₁₆". Clip corners and curves, and turn right side out. Press. Hand-stitch opening closed.

6. Referring to photo on page 4 and block layout on page 9, position Marigold pocket on purse. Tuck raw edge of Marigold flap from step 4 under top edge of pocket. Edge-stitch along top, bottom, and sides of pocket. Fold flap over pocket and sew button through all layers.

7. For Primrose Block handle refer to Quick-Fuse Appliqué on page 109 and fuse ¾" x 12½" piece of lightweight fusible web to wrong side of Fabric B green scrap. Cut one ½" x 8" piece and two ½" x 2" pieces. Referring to photo on page 4 and block layout on page 11, fuse pieces to block to make purse handle.

8. Referring to Quick-Fuse Appliqué on page 109, photo on page 4, and block layout on page 11, cut 6" x 8" Fabric D piece rounding corners and fuse to purse with lightweight fusible web. Finish fused pieces with machine satin stitch or other decorative stitching as desired.

9. Turn under ¼" on all sides of 5½" x 4⅝" Fabric D piece. Press. Center on one 5¾" x 4¾" Fabric D piece and edge-stitch smaller piece in place on all sides. Place this unit, right sides together, with remaining 5¾" x 4¾" Fabric D piece. Using ¼"-wide seam, sew around edges, leaving 3" opening for turning. Clip corners, turn, and press. Hand-stitch opening closed.

10. Trace Primrose Flap template (page 12) on wrong side of 3" x 6" Fabric D piece. Place right sides together with matching 3" x 6" Fabric D piece and batting. Stitch on drawn line, leaving top edge free. Cut out flap, trim batting close to stitching, and trim seam allowance to ³⁄₁₆". Clip curves, turn right side out, and press.

11. Referring to photo on page 4 and block layout on page 11, position units from step 9 and 10 on purse. Tuck raw edge of flap approximately ¼" under top edge of unit from step 9. Edge-stitch piece along all sides. Fold flap down and sew a button through all layers.

LAYERING & FINISHING

1. Cut backing in half crosswise. Sew pieces together to make one 47" x 80" (approximate) backing piece. Press and trim backing to 47" x 47". Arrange and baste backing, batting, and top together, referring to Layering the Quilt on page 110.

2. Hand or machine quilt as desired.

3. Sew 2¾" x 42" binding strips end-to-end to make one continuous 2¾"-wide strip. Refer to Binding the Quilt on page 111 and bind quilt to finish.

MAKING THE LEAVES

Leaf patterns are marked with a vein line. This will be used later as the stitching line when attaching leaves to block or attach as desired.

1. Refer to Quick-Fuse Appliqué on page 109. Fuse two pieces of 4½" x 8" leaf fabric wrong sides together with heavy-weight fusible web. Using Star Flower Leaf template (page 12), trace four leaves on fused fabric. Cut on traced lines. Using temporary fabric marker, trace vein lines on leaves. Label these Star Flower Leaves.

2. Referring to step 1, use Bell Flower Top Leaf template (page 11) and two 11" x 2" leaf fabrics to fuse, mark and cut six leaf sections. Label these Bell Flower Top Leaves.

3. Using Bell Flower Lower Leaf template (page 11), trace six leaves on wrong side 4" x 12" leaf fabric, leaving ½" between leaves. Place marked fabric with matching 4" x 12" leaf fabric, right sides together, over batting scrap. Stitch on drawn lines. Cut out leaves, trim batting close to stitching, and trim seams allowance to ³⁄₁₆". Clip points and curves. Carefully slit leaf backs, turn right side out, and press. Using temporary fabric marker, trace vein lines on leaves. Label these Bell Flower Lower Leaves.

4. Referring to step 1, use Marigold Leaf template (page 11) and two 3" x 6" leaf fabrics to fuse, mark and cut five leaves. Label these Marigold Leaves.

5. Referring to step 3, use Primrose Leaf template (page 11), and two 3" x 16" leaf fabrics to mark, stitch, trim, turn and press, making eight leaves. Mark veins and label these Primrose Leaves.

MAKING FLOWERS
Star Flower Block

*Star Flowers are formed using a technique developed by Kumiko Sudo and detailed in her book, **Folded Flowers: Fabric Origami with a Twist of Silk Ribbon**, Breckling Press 2002.*

1. Using Star Flower template (page 12), trace five flowers on wrong side of Fabric A piece that matches block background. Place one marked fabric right side together with Star Flower Fabric. Stitch ⅛" inside drawn lines. Cut on drawn lines. Clip corners. Carefully slit Fabric A, turn right side out, and press. Make five.

2. Place unit from step 1 slit side down. Fold each point to center as shown. Tack in place.

3. Fold edges of each section back to open petals as shown. Tack sides of petals together about ⅜" from flower center to reveal star. Sew decorative bead in center. Make five.

4. Wrap ⅜"-wide cotton filler cord with 3½" x 14" Star Flower Purse Handle bias strip (right side out). Wrap fabric over ends of cording prior to stitching. Using zipper or cording foot, stitch close to cord. Trim seam close to stitching.

5. Referring to Couching Technique on page 111 and block layout, stitch yarn to block for stems. Arrange flowers, leaves, and handle on block and hand stitch in place.

Bell Flower Block

1. Fold 2" x 4" piece of Bell Flower fabric in half lengthwise, wrong sides together. Press. Unfold and sew 2" ends right sides together using ⅛"-wide seam to make a ring. Finger press seam open. Refold on pressed lines. Using basting stitch, sew ⅛" from raw edges. Insert top

leaf so only straight edge shows through basted opening. Pull thread tightly to gather and tack to secure. Turn flower right side out to show leaves. Make six flowers.

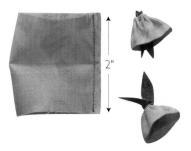

2. Referring to Quick-Fuse Appliqué on page 109, fuse two 7" stem fabric squares wrong sides together, with heavyweight fusible web. Cut on bias two ¼" x 5" and two ¼" x 4" strips for flower stems.

3. Referring to photo on page 4 and block layout, arrange stems, flowers and lower leaves (slit side down) on block. Set aside one leaf to be attached after handle is added. To give extra dimension, pinch bottom section of a few leaves. Hand stitch in place.

4. Using Purse Tab template (page 12), trace two on wrong side of Fabric C, leaving ½" between tracings. Place marked fabric and matching-size scraps right sides together over batting scrap. Stitch on drawn lines. Cut out Tabs, trim batting close to stitching, and seam allowance to ³⁄₁₆". Clip points and curves. Carefully slit back and turn right side out. Press.

5. Refer to block layout and using a 10" piece of decorative cording for handle, arrange handle and Tabs on block, making sure Tabs enclose handle ends. Hand appliqué in place and stitch remaining leaf to block, overlapping handle.

Marigold Block

1. Refer to Quick-Fuse Appliqué on page 109. Trace 1" x 8¾" rectangle on paper side of fusible web. Fuse web to Marigold Purse Trim Appliqué Fabric and cut. Refer to block layout to position and fuse. Finish edges as desired.

2. Using Marigold Center template (page 11), wrap strands of green embroidery floss around 1⅞" side of template approximately 10 times. Use a 6" piece of floss to tie floss loops together as shown then remove floss from template.

3. Cut one 2" x 30" Marigold Flower strip, place right side down, and fold long raw edges to meet at center. Press. Fold in half lengthwise and press. Strip should measure ½" wide.

4. With pencil, mark bottom edge of strip at 1" intervals. Mark top edge at 1" intervals starting ½" from end.

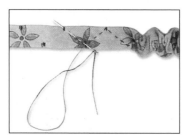

5. Beginning with top edge, use ⅛"-long stitches to hand-baste from top mark to bottom mark and back to next top mark, forming a zigzag pattern. Gently pull thread tightly, gathering fabric to approximately one-third of original length, forming a row of petal-like shapes. Knot end of thread.

6. To make flower, coil three of the petal shapes to form center. Secure in place. Fold floss loops from step 1 in half and insert into coil center. Stitch in place. Continue coiling gathered strip around center until flower is desired size. Secure and tuck under raw ends. Trim floss to desired length. Repeat steps 3-6 to make three flowers.

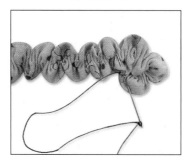

7. Referring to photo on page 4 and layout, use one long stitch and silk ribbon to make each stem.

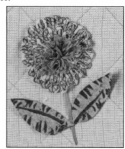

8. Referring to photo on page 4 and layout, arrange flowers and leaves on block and stitch in place. Using 12" long braid for handle, arrange on block and trim as needed, turning under ends.

POCKETBOOK FULL OF POSiES WALL QUiLT
Finished size: 41½" x 41½"
Photo: *page 4*

Primrose Block

1. Fold 2" x 16" strip of Primrose Flower Fabric lengthwise, wrong sides together. Using Primrose Stitching Pattern, mark five sections on fabric as shown.

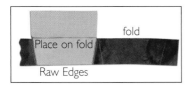

2. Beginning with folded edge, use ⅛"-long stitches to hand-baste from top mark to ⅛" from raw edge, across raw edge, and back to next top mark, forming pattern shown. Gently pull thread tightly, gathering fabric to form five petal-like shapes as shown and fasten thread.

3. Wrap coil to form a five-petal flower, stitch to secure, and tuck under raw ends. Stitch center together and sew button to center of flower. Repeat steps to make four flowers.

4. Referring to photo on page 4 and layout, arrange flowers and leaves (slit side down) on block as shown. Stitch in place.

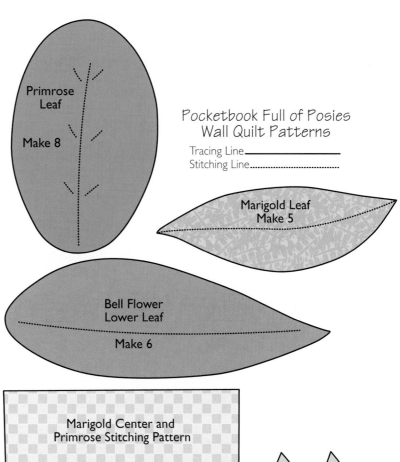

Primrose
Leaf

Make 8

Pocketbook Full of Posies Wall Quilt Patterns

Tracing Line _____

Stitching Line ·····················

Marigold Leaf
Make 5

Bell Flower
Lower Leaf

Make 6

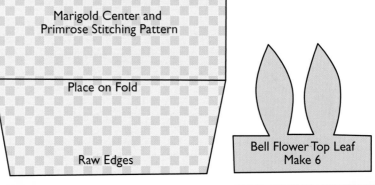

Marigold Center and
Primrose Stitching Pattern

Place on Fold

Raw Edges

Bell Flower Top Leaf
Make 6

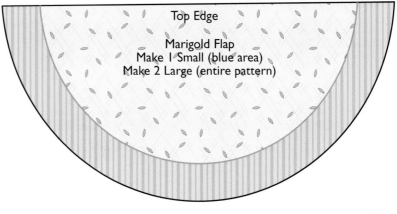

Top Edge

Marigold Flap
Make 1 Small (blue area)
Make 2 Large (entire pattern)

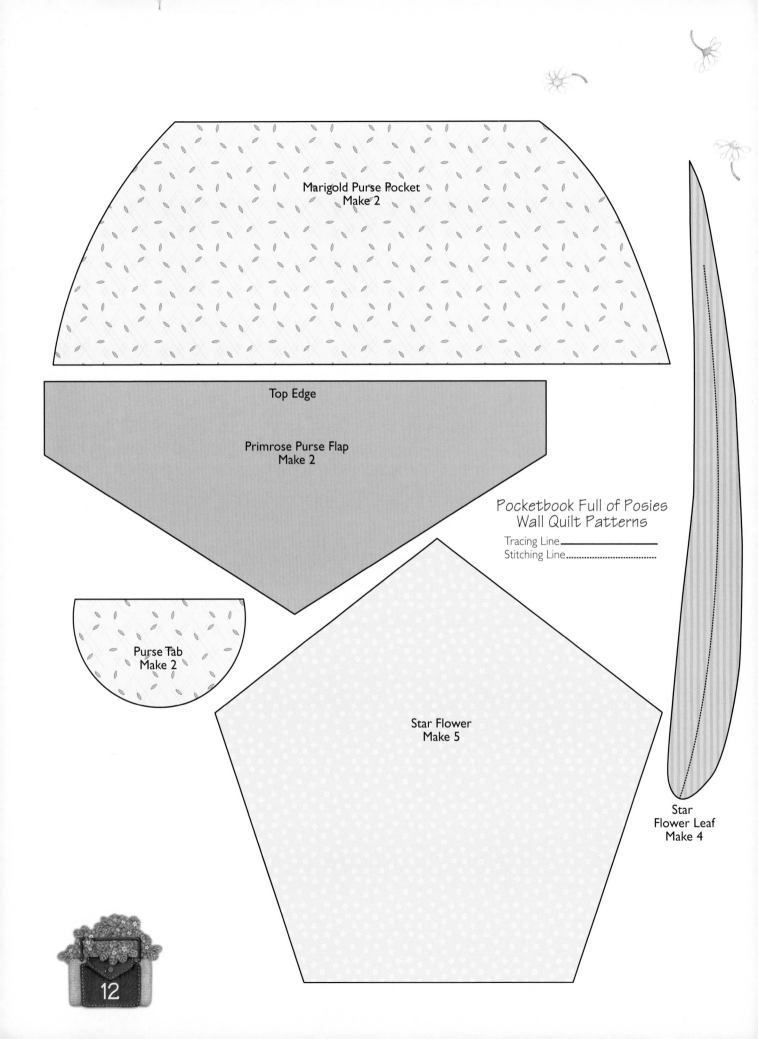

Marigold Purse Pocket
Make 2

Top Edge

Primrose Purse Flap
Make 2

Pocketbook Full of Posies
Wall Quilt Patterns

Tracing Line————————
Stitching Line..........................

Purse Tab
Make 2

Star Flower
Make 5

Star
Flower Leaf
Make 4

12

Plant a Pocketbook

Add a whimsical touch to your patio by using an old purse as a fun flower container.

MATERIALS NEEDED

Purse or Tote Bag
Primrose Flowers - ⅛ yard
  Three 2" x 16" Fabric Strips
Primrose Leaves - ⅛ yard
Three Yellow Buttons
Assorted Plants in Plastic Pots

MAKING THE TOTE

We chose a rugged straw tote, but any cute and colorful purse will do. Just put smaller plants in a small purse!

1. Refer to Pocketbook Full of Posies, Primrose Block, on page 11, steps 1-3, to make three fabric flowers.

2. Refer to Making the Leaves on page 8, step 5, to make four Primrose Leaves.

3. Place Primroses and Leaves on tote where desired and hand-stitch or glue in place. If desired, sew on additional buttons for an added whimsical accent.

4. If you want to save the purse planter from year to year, do not plant directly into the tote. Instead, keep flowers and plants in plastic pots. Line the tote with several large plastic bags. If tote is deep, place several bricks of florist foam in the bottom to raise potted plants to an appropriate height.

5. Water plants regularly, being careful not to let water accumulate in the bottom of plastic-lined tote.

6. At the end of the season, remove plants and store tote.

A plant-filled pocketbook would be a fun gift for a favorite gardener, or as a birthday or Mother's Day gift for a special lady.

13

COLOR SPECTRUM

82½" x 82½" • Quilt

Whoever sleeps under this glorious quilt is all but guaranteed technicolor dreams! It's a fabric lover's delight ... the perfect opportunity to dive into that rainbow of fabric you've been collecting. The blocks are divided diagonally for a light-and-shadow effect, and you'll love the easy way they're constructed.

FABRIC REQUIREMENTS & CUTTING INSTRUCTIONS

Read all instructions before beginning and use ¼"-wide seam allowances throughout. Read Cutting Strips and Pieces on page 108 prior to cutting fabrics.

Color Spectrum Quilt 82½" x 82½"	FIRST CUT		SECOND CUT	
	Number of Strips or Pieces	Dimensions	Number of Pieces	Dimensions
Note: After piecing the blocks there will be a few extra remaining pieces. This will allow a play of color in block placement.				
Fabric A Black ½ yard each of nine fabrics	1* 4*	4" x 42" 2¼" x 42" *Cut for each fabric	6* 12* 12*	4" squares 2¼" x 7½" 2¼" x 4"
Fabric B Light Gold ⅙ yard each of three fabrics	1* 1*	2½" x 42" 2¼" x 42" *Cut for each fabric	9* 6* 6*	2½" squares 2¼" x 4" 2¼" squares
Fabric C Medium Gold ⅛ yard	1	2¼" x 42"	2 2 2 2	2¼" x 7½" 2¼" x 5¾" 2¼" x 4" 2¼" squares
Fabric D Dark Gold ¼ yard each of three fabrics	1* 2*	2½" x 42" 2¼" x 42" *Cut for each fabric	6* 3* 6*	2½" squares 2¼" x 7½" 2¼" x 5¾"
Fabric E Light Orange ⅙ yard each of three fabrics	3* 1*	2½" squares 2¼" x 42" *Cut for each fabric	6* 6*	2¼" x 4" 2¼" squares
Fabric F Dark Orange ¼ yard each of three fabrics	3* 2*	2½" squares 2¼" x 42" *Cut for each fabric	3* 6*	2¼" x 7½" 2¼" x 5¾"
Fabric G Light Blue ¼ yard each of three fabrics	3* 2*	2½" squares 2¼" x 42" *Cut for each fabric	7* 7*	2¼" x 4" 2¼" squares"
Fabric H Dark Blue ¼ yard each of three fabrics	3* 2*	2½" squares 2¼" x 42" *Cut for each fabric	4* 7*	2¼" x 7½" 2¼" x 5¾"
Fabric I Light Purple ⅛ yard each of three fabrics	1*	2½" x 42" *Cut for each fabric	2* 2* 3*	2½" squares 2¼" x 4" 2¼" squares
Fabric J Medium Purple ⅛ yard	1	2½" x 42"	1 1 2 2	2½" square 2¼" x 7½" 2¼" x 5¾" 2¼" x 4"
Fabric K Dark Purple ⅛ yard each of three fabrics	1*	2½" x 42" *Cut for each fabric	2* 1* 2*	2½" squares 2¼" x 7½" 2¼" x 5¾"
Fabric L Light Green ¼ yard each of three fabrics	2* 2*	2½" squares 2¼" x 42" *Cut for each fabric	7* 7*	2¼" x 4" 2¼" squares

Color Spectrum Quilt continued	FIRST CUT		SECOND CUT	
	Number of Strips or Pieces	Dimensions	Number of Pieces	Dimensions
Fabric M Dark Green ¼ yard each of three fabrics	1* 2*	2½" square 2¼" x 42" *Cut for each fabric	4* 7*	2¼" x 7½" 2¼" x 5¾"
Fabric N Light Red ⅙ yard each of three fabrics	1* 1*	2½" square 2¼" x 42" *Cut for each fabric	6* 6*	2¼" x 4" 2¼" squares
Fabric O Dark Red ¼ yard each of three fabrics	1* 2*	2½" square 2¼" x 42" *Cut for each fabric	3* 6*	2¼" x 7½" 2¼" x 5¾"
BORDERS				
First Border ⅜ yard	7	1½" x 42"		
Second Border ⅓ yard	7	1¼" x 42"		
Third Border & Outside Border 1¼ yards	8 8	3" x 42" (Outside Border) 2" x 42" (Third Border)		
Fourth Border ½ yard	8	1½" x 42"		
Fifth Border ⅝ yard	8	2" x 42"		
Binding ¾ yard	9	2¾" x 42"		
Backing - 7½ yards Batting - 90" x 90"				

Fabric Tip: The center of this quilt can be made easily out of fabric fat quarters. You will need the following:

Fabric A - Eighteen fat quarters
Cut three 4" squares, six 2¼" x 7½" pieces, and six 2½" x 4" pieces from each fat quarter.

Fabrics B, D, E, F, G, H, I, K, L, M, N, and O - Three fat quarters for each fabric in assorted shades
Cut pieces listed in chart.

Fabrics C and J - One fat quarter of each
Cut pieces listed in chart.

GETTING STARTED

This scrappy quilt includes one-hundred 7" square (unfinished) blocks made in seven different colors and a variety of configurations. That may sound like a lot, but all are constructed from just two simple, pieced units, and our quick and easy methods make piecing them a breeze. The overall quilt is pieced in four large sections and then sewn together like one giant block.

Before you begin stitching, sort fabric pieces by color: gold, orange, blue, purple, green, red, and black. Next, sort the pieces of each color by size: 2½" squares, 2¼" squares, 2¼" x 4" pieces, and so on. This will make it easy to piece the blocks—just pull a piece of the correct color in the appropriate size—and the results will be good and scrappy. (Set the 2½" squares aside to be used in Making the Blocks, page 17.)

Refer to Accurate Seam Allowance on page 108. Whenever possible, use the Assembly Line Method on page 108. Press seams in direction of arrows.

MAKING THE COLOR UNITS

1. Sew one 2¼" gold square to a contrasting 2¼" gold square as shown. Press. Make eight.

Make 8

2. Sew one 2¼" x 4" gold piece to one unit from step 1. Press. Make eight.

Make 8

3. Sew one 2¼" x 4" gold piece to one unit from step 2 as shown. Press. Make eight.

Make 8

4. Sew one 2¼" x 5¾" gold piece to one unit from step 3 as shown. Press. Make eight.

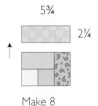

Make 8

5. Sew one 2¼" x 5¾" gold piece to one unit from step 4 as shown. Press. Make eight.

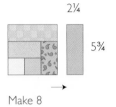

Make 8

6. Sew one 2¼" x 7½" gold piece to one unit from step 5 as shown. Press. Make eight.

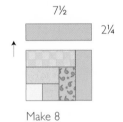

Make 8

7. Repeat steps 1-6 using the appropriately-colored fabrics to make eight orange blocks, eight red blocks, ten green blocks, ten blue blocks, and four purple blocks.

Make 8 in assorted golds

Make 8 in assorted oranges

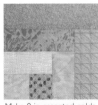
Make 8 in assorted reds

Make 10 in assorted greens

Make 10 in assorted blues

Make 4 in assorted purples

MAKING THE BLACK UNITS

1. Sew one 4" Fabric A square between two contrasting 2¼" x 4" Fabric A pieces as shown. Press. Make fifty.

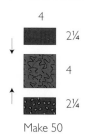

4
2¼
4
2¼

Make 50

2. Sew one unit from step 1 between two 2¼" x 7½" Fabric A pieces as shown. Press. Make fifty.

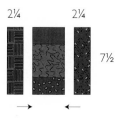

2¼   2¼
7½

Make 50

MAKING THE BLOCKS

1. Draw diagonal line on wrong side of one gold Color Unit, noting direction of drawn line to seams. Place marked unit and one black unit right sides together as shown. Sew a scant ¼" away from drawn line on both sides to make half-square triangles. Make eight. Cut on drawn line. Press. Square to 7". This will make sixteen half-square triangle blocks.

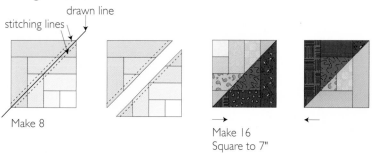

drawn line
stitching lines
Make 8
Make 16
Square to 7"

2. Repeat step 1, using each color unit and forty black units to make the following; sixteen orange/black blocks, sixteen red/black blocks, twenty green/black blocks, twenty blue/black blocks, and eight purple/black blocks.

3. Draw diagonal line on wrong side of one remaining black unit. Place marked unit and unmarked black unit right sides together as shown. Sew a scant ¼" away from drawn line on both sides to make half-square triangles. Make two. Cut on drawn line. Press. Square to 7". This makes four half-square triangle blocks.

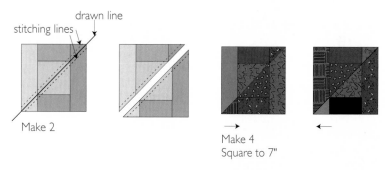

drawn line
stitching lines
Make 2
Make 4
Square to 7"

4. Refer to Quick Corner Triangles on page 108. Sew one 2½" Fabric N or Fabric O square to one unit from step 3 as shown. Press. Make four.

N or O = 2½ x 2½
Black Block
Make 4

17

5. Making a quick corner triangle unit, sew one 2½" Fabric L or Fabric M square to one gold/black unit. Press. Make eight. Repeat to sew one 2½" Fabric B or Fabric D square to one gold/black unit. Press. Make eight.

L or M = 2½ x 2½
Gold Block
Make 8

B or D = 2½ x 2½
Gold Block
Make 8

6. Making a quick corner triangle unit, sew one 2½" Fabric I, J, or K square to one orange/black unit as shown. Press. Make twelve. Repeat to sew 2½" squares to each unit from step 2 in the combinations and quantities shown.

I, J or K = 2½ x 2½
Orange Block
Make 12

E or F = 2½ x 2½
Orange Block
Make 4

G or H = 2½ x 2½
Red Block
Make 16

B or D = 2½ x 2½
Green Block
Make 20

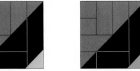

B or D = 2½ x 2½
Blue Block
Make 8

E or F = 2½ x 2½
Blue Block
Make 12

B or D = 2½ x 2½
Purple Block
Make 8

ASSEMBLY

1. Arrange blocks in five rows of five blocks each, placing them exactly as shown. Sew blocks into rows. Press. Make four of each row.

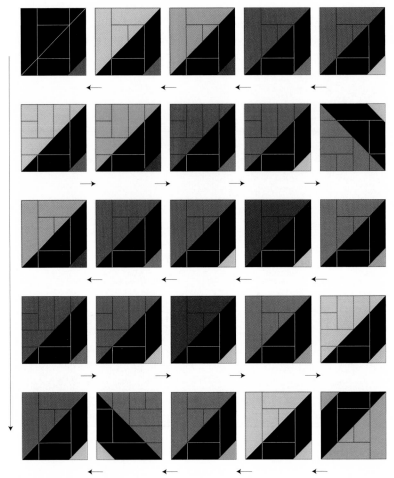

Make 4

2. Referring to diagram in step 1, arrange rows and sew together as shown to make quarter section. Press. Make four quarter sections. Refer to photo on page 14 and layout. Arrange and sew quarter sections together. Press.

BORDERS

1. Sew 1½" x 42" First Border strips end-to-end to make one continuous 1½"-wide strip. Refer to Adding the Borders on page 110. Measure quilt through center from side to side. Cut two 1½"-wide strips to that measurement. Sew to top and bottom of quilt. Press seams toward border.

2. Measure quilt through center from top to bottom, including borders just added. Cut two 1½"-wide First Border strips to that measurement. Sew to sides of quilt. Press.

3. Refer to steps 1 and 2 to measure, trim, and sew 1¼"-wide Second Border strips, 2"-wide Third Border strips, 1½"-wide Fourth Border strips, 2"-wide Fifth Border strips, and 3"-wide Outside Border strips to top, bottom, and sides of quilt. Press seams toward each newly added border strip.

LAYERING & FINISHING

1. Cut backing crosswise into three equal pieces. Sew pieces together to make one 90" x 120" (approximate) backing piece. Press and trim to 90" x 90".

2. Arrange and baste backing, batting, and top together, referring to Layering the Quilt on page 110.

3. Hand or machine quilt as desired.

4. Sew 2¾" x 42" binding strips end-to-end to make one continuous 2¾"-wide strip. Refer to Binding the Quilt on page 111 and bind quilt to finish.

COLOR SPECTRUM QUILT
Finished size: 82½" x 82½"
Photo: page 14

IN THE LiMELiGHT

47" x 47" • Table Quilt

Every day will feel like summer when you dress the table in this carefree, citrus-inspired topper. The refreshing colors and larger-than-life appliqués are enhanced by our own polka dot-painted fabric. Our flavor of the day is lime, but you could easily substitute another color to suit your personal palette!

FABRIC REQUIREMENTS & CUTTING INSTRUCTIONS

Read all instructions before beginning and use ¼"-wide seam allowances throughout. Read Cutting Strips and Pieces on page 108 prior to cutting fabrics.

In the Limelight Table Quilt 47" x 47"	FIRST CUT	
	Number of Strips or Pieces	Dimensions
Fabric A *Background* ½ yard each of two fabrics	1*	15½" square
		*Cut for each fabric
Fabric B Background & Fourth Border 1½ yards (for painting fabric) OR 1⅓ yards (non-painted)	4	48" x 6" (Border)
	2	15½" squares
		OR
	2	15½" squares
	5	5¾" x 42" (Border)
Fabric C Lime Sections & Medium Rind Appliqués 1⅛ yards		1⅝"-wide bias strips cut from 16" square
Fabric D Dark Rind ½ yard		1⅝"-wide bias strips cut from 16" square
Fabric E Light Rind ½ yard		1"-wide bias strips cut from 16" square
BORDERS		
First & Outside Border ⅓ yard	9	1" x 42"
Second Border ⅛ yard	4	¾" x 42"
Third Border & Binding ⅔ yard	5	2¾" x 42" (Binding)
	4	2" x 42"

Backing - 3 yards
Batting - 52" x 52"
Lime Center Appliqué - Scraps
Lightweight Fusible Web -1½ yards
Acrylic Paints - Orange, lime green, & yellow green
Sponge Pouncer (Available at art or craft stores with stencil supplies)
Fabric Painting Medium
Compass Points & Yardstick

GETTING STARTED

This quilt features four 15½" (unfinished) appliqué blocks and a whimsical painted polka dot border. The lime rinds are made by sewing bias strips together to make a strip set, cutting the strip set into segments, and sewing the segments into tubes. This makes it easy to curve the rinds into shape and appliqué them to the blocks without turning under any raw edges. The lime centers and lime sections are done with easy Quick-Fuse Appliqué.

The border fabric is painted with acrylic paints before the border strips are sewn to the quilt.

MARKING BACKGROUND SQUARES

Mark each 15½" Fabric A and B background square to indicate placement of rind and lime appliqués. Use compass points and a yardstick to draw arcs. Mark lightly or use a removable marker for all markings.

1. Draw a square ¼" inside raw edges of 15½" Fabric A square to indicate 15" finished block size.

2. Set compass points so points are 14⅞" apart. Place point of compass at one corner of drawn (inside) square and draw an arc as shown in step 3. Reset compass placing points 12⅞" apart and draw second arc 2" inside first arc.

3. Use patterns on page 24 to make templates for Lime Section and Lime Center. Place Lime Center template (position 1) ⅛" from corner of drawn square as shown and trace. Place Lime Section template (position 2) ⅝" from side of drawn square and with curved edge on inside arc, trace. Repeat to position and trace second lime section on adjacent side of square (position 3). Center middle Lime Section between side Lime Sections with curved edge on arc and trace (position 4).

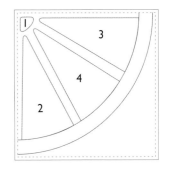

4. Repeat steps 1-3 to mark remaining 15½" Fabric A and B squares.

MAKING THE BLOCKS

1. Cut enough 1⅝"-wide bias strips from 16" Fabric C square to equal 105". Sew strips end-to-end to make one continuous 1⅝"-wide bias strip. Press. Repeat to cut and sew 1"-wide Fabric E bias strips and 1⅝"-wide Fabric D bias strips to equal 105".

2. Sew 1"-wide Fabric E bias strip between 1⅝"-wide Fabric C, and 1⅝"-wide Fabric D bias strips from step 1 along lengthwise seams. Press seams away from center strip. Cut strip set into four 25"-long segments.

3. Fold each segment from step 2 lengthwise, **wrong sides together**, and sew with ¼"-wide seam to make a tube. Make 1¼" x 25" template from sturdy cardboard and insert in tube. (Cut a point at one end of template to make it slip in more easily.) Center seam you've just sewn over back of template, align strips on front, and press seam to one side as shown. Remove template and press again. Use template to press remaining three tubes.

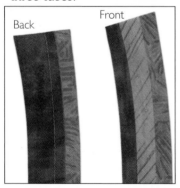

Back   Front

ADDING APPLIQUÉS

Refer to appliqué instructions on page 109. Our instructions are for Quick-Fuse Appliqué, but if you prefer hand appliqué, add ¼"-wide seam allowances.

1. Use Lime Center template and assorted green scraps to cut four Lime Centers. Use Lime Section template and Fabric C to cut twelve lime sections.

2. Position Lime Center and Lime Section Appliqués on each marked background block. Fuse appliqués in place and finish with machine satin stitch or other decorative stitching as desired.

Tip: To shape rind section into an arc, use compass points to draw 14⅞" arc on paper. Spray rind section with spray starch, place on marked paper, and press. Form rind arc along drawn line.

3. Refer to photos below and on page 20. Align tubes along drawn outside curve line on background fabric. Align Fabric C edge of tube with outside of Fabric B backgrounds and align Fabric D edge on Fabric A backgrounds. Pin. Trim ends of tube if needed, and use blind hem stitch to appliqué in place.

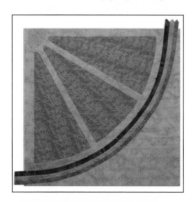

ASSEMBLY

1. Refer to photo on page 20 and layout. Arrange blocks in two rows of two blocks each.

2. Sew blocks together into rows. Press seams in opposite directions from row to row.

3. Sew rows together. Press.

PAINTING POLKA DOT FABRIC

Note: Before starting on the fabric, practice with the pouncer and each color of paint on a piece of paper first, to get a feel for how far apart to place dots and how to get uniformly round polka dots. We used the sponge part of the pouncer for large dots and the wooden end of the pouncer for small dots. When ready to paint the fabric, paint one border piece first to make sure you like the effect, then use that border piece as a model for the other three.

1. Cover long table with cardboard or plastic (paint will seep through fabric). Arrange border strips side by side on the covered table and tape short edges to table to hold pieces in place.

2. Following directions on Fabric Painting Medium, mix Fabric Medium with lime green paint on plastic plate or palette.

3. Rub sponge pouncer in paint, making sure to cover entire bottom of pouncer. Blot pouncer on palette or plastic plate, then randomly sponge lime green dots onto fabric strip. Rotate handle of pouncer slightly from side to side to make sure edges of each dot transfer.

Paint several dots before refilling pouncer with paint. Small bubbles may appear in painted dots, but paint will dry just fine. Wash out pouncer and allow fabric to dry.

4. Repeat process from step 2, making large dots with yellow-green paint. Allow to dry.

5. Use the wooden end of pouncer to make small dots. Mix Fabric Medium with orange paint and dip wooden end into orange paint mixture. Keeping the wooden stick straight up as shown, make a small dot on fabric. Repeat, randomly placing orange dots. Rinse wooden handle and allow fabric to dry.

6. Repeat step 5, adding lime green and yellow green small dots to the border fabric.

7. Set paint as directed on Fabric Painting Medium. Since color may bleed when fabric is iron-set, place a cloth or paper under fabric to protect ironing board.

8. Cut fabric into 5¾"-wide strips.

BORDERS

1. Refer to Adding the Borders on page 110. Measure quilt through center from side to side. Cut two 1" x 42" First Border strips to that measurement. Sew to top and bottom of quilt. Press seams toward border strips.

2. Measure quilt through center from top to bottom, including borders just added. Cut two 1"-wide First Border strips to that measurement. Sew to sides of quilt. Press.

IN THE LiMELiGHT TABLE QUiLT
Finished size: *47" x 47"*
Photo: *page 20*

3. Refer to steps 1 and 2 to measure, trim, and sew
¾"-wide Second Border strips, 2"-wide Third Border
strips, and 5¾" Fourth Border strips to top, bottom,
and sides of quilt. Press seams toward newly added
border strips.

4. Sew 1"-wide Outside Border strips end-to-end to
make one continuous 1"-wide strip. Refer to steps
1 and 2 to measure, trim, and sew 1"-wide
Outside Border strips to top, bottom, and sides of
quilt. Press seams towards Outside Border strips.

LAYERING & FINISHING

1. Cut backing in half crosswise. Sew pieces
together to make one 54" x 80"
(approximate) backing piece. Press and trim
to 54" x 54".

2. Arrange and baste backing, batting, and
top together, referring to Layering the
Quilt on page 110.

3. Hand or machine quilt as desired.

4. Sew 2¾" x 42" binding strips
end-to-end to make one continuous
2¾"-wide strip. Refer to Binding
the Quilt on page 111 and bind
quilt to finish.

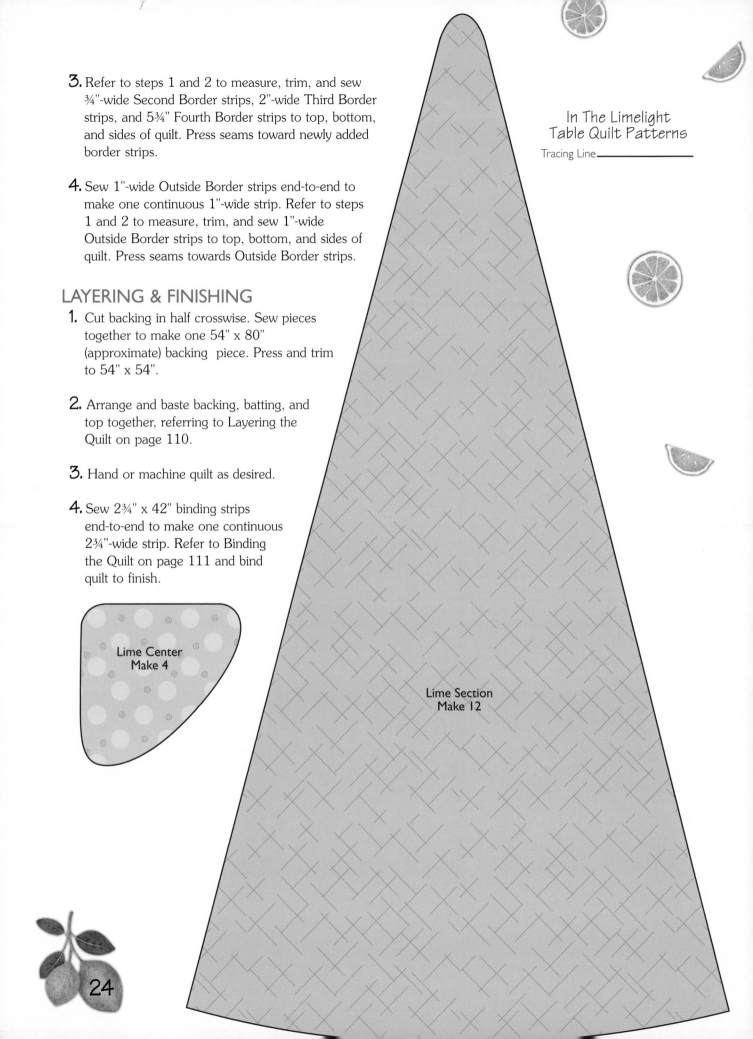

In The Limelight
Table Quilt Patterns
Tracing Line _____

Lime Center
Make 4

Lime Section
Make 12

24

Lemon-Lime Napkin & Ring

Playful two-color napkins are the perfect complement for In the Limelight Table Quilt.
Tiny pom-poms add whimsy while painted napkin rings provide polka dot dash!

MATERIALS NEEDED
(for two napkins and rings)

Yellow Fabric - ½ yard
  Two 17" squares
Green Fabric - ½ yard
  Two 17" squares
Small Pom-Pom Trim - 3¾ yards
Two Wooden Napkin Rings
Sandpaper
Acrylic Craft Paints - Yellow, orange, light green, & medium green
Paint Brush
Sponge Pouncer
Matte Craft Varnish

Finished Napkin size:
16½" x 16½"

MAKING THE NAPKINS

1. Baste pom-poms on the right side, along edges, of each Green Fabric square making sure pom-poms face toward center of napkin.

2. Place each green square right sides together with a Yellow Fabric square and pin, being careful that pom-poms are facing toward center of fabric.

3. Using a zipper foot and sewing a ½"-wide seam, sew along each edge, being careful to completely enclose the pom-pom tape in the seam. Leave a 3" opening for turning.

4. Clip corners, turn right side out, and press. Hand-sew the opening closed.

MAKING THE NAPKIN RINGS

1. Sand wooden napkin rings lightly and remove residue with a damp cloth.

2. Paint each napkin ring yellow. Two or more coats of paint may be required for good coverage. Allow to dry completely between each paint application.

3. Refer to In the Limelight Quilt, painting Polka Dot Fabric, pages 22-23, steps 3-6, to paint polka dots on napkin rings using the sponge pouncer. Fabric Medium is not required for this project.

4. When thoroughly dry, apply matte varnish to napkin rings.

LUSCIOUS LIME
FLOOR CLOTH

42" Round • Floor Cloth

Set the scene for a citrus fiesta on your patio with this luscious lime floor cloth. Easy painting techniques make this floor cloth as fun to make as it is festive! If desired, use as a weatherproof table covering for a splash of originality.

MATERIALS NEEDED:

Pre-Primed Floorcloth Canvas*
(52" wide) - 1¼ yards

Acrylic Craft Paints - Ivory,
lime green, yellow-green,
yellow, gold

Compass Points & Yardstick

See-Through Ruler with
Marked 30° Angle

Assorted Paintbrushes

Sea Sponge

Checkerboard Stencil

Pencil & Eraser

Satin or Matte Finish Acrylic
Craft Varnish

> **Because of the round shape,*
> *look for pre-primed floorcloth*
> *canvas that does not require a*
> *hemmed edge.*

MAKING THE FLOOR CLOTH

1. Read all instructions before beginning. Cut a 45" square piece from the pre-primed floorcloth canvas. Paint the entire piece with ivory paint. Allow to dry.

2. Mark the center of the canvas piece. This will be used in steps 3-5. Using a yard stick, set compass points 21" apart and draw a 42" circle on the painted-side of the canvas.

3. Referring to diagram, use the same center point to draw four circles inside the 42" circle as indicated below. Draw a 3" diameter circle in the center.

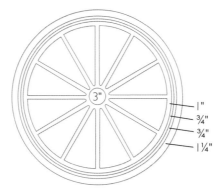

4. Using the yardstick, lightly draw two lines to divide circle into quarters, making sure lines are perpendicular.

5. Using see-through ruler, line up 30° angle with one line and lightly draw a line from center point to inside circle to form wedge shape. Continue drawing lines at 30° angles around the circle, lining up 30° angle with each newly drawn line, until circle has twelve equal wedge shapes. Mark ½" points on both sides of each line then draw lines to form 1" veins between each wedge section. Erase first set of 30° angle lines. Use pencil to round off narrow end of each wedge as shown in photo. Touch up ivory paint, if needed.

6. Use Scotch™ Magic™ Tape to mask off 1" ivory veins. Paint each wedge section yellow-green. Two or more coats of paint may be needed for good coverage. Allow paint to dry thoroughly between each application.

7. Wet sea sponge and wring thoroughly. Place a small amount of lime green paint on palette or plastic plate. Dip sea sponge in lime green paint, blot several times on paper towel, then sponge onto the yellow-green painted section using a tapping motion. Apply lightly for a slightly stippled effect. Allow to dry. Remove tape.

8. Referring to photograph, paint outside and third circle yellow-green. Paint second circle and 3" center yellow. Allow each circle to dry thoroughly before painting the next circle. Use stencil and gold paint to add checks to center. Referring to photo, use a ½" flat brush to paint lime green stripes on outside circle.

9. Cut out lime slice floor cloth on 42" circle line. Use a clean damp sponge and gently wipe the surface to clean off any residue. Apply a thin coat of acrylic varnish over entire floorcloth. Let surface dry and then repeat process, applying 3-5 more coats. Allow to dry thoroughly.

FRIENDSHIP FLOWERS

41" x 41" • Wall Quilt

What better way to celebrate the special friendships that bloom in your life than by making an extra-special quilt? This colorful, flower-filled wall piece fills the bill perfectly! You'll love the garden-fresh mix of colors and prints…and the quick-piecing techniques that make construction so-o-o-o easy.

FABRIC REQUIREMENTS & CUTTING INSTRUCTIONS

Read all instructions before beginning and use ¼"-wide seam allowances throughout. Read Cutting Strips and Pieces on page 108 prior to cutting fabrics.

Friendship Flowers Wall Quilt 41" x 41"	FIRST CUT		SECOND CUT	
	Number of Strips or Pieces	Dimensions	Number of Pieces	Dimensions
Fabric A *Background* 1⅓ yards *(If machine embroidering)* OR ⅞ yard *(Cut four 2½"-wide strips instead of two 15"-wide strips)*	2	15" x 42"	4	2½" x 10½"**
			4	2½" x 9½"**
	1	12¼" x 42"	2	12¼" squares *cut once diagonally*
	1	2½" x 42"	16	2½" squares
	2	1½" x 42"	4	1½" x 2½"
			32	1½" squares
	**Sizes to be cut for piecing after embroidery.			
Fabric B *Medallion Flower Med Purple* ⅙ yard	1	3½" x 42"	4	3½" squares
Fabric C *Medallion Center Scrap*	4	1½" "fussy cut" squares		
Fabric D *Medallion Accent* ⅛ yard	1	1½" x 42"	16	1½" squares
Fabric E *Medallion Flower Lt Purple* ⅙ yard	1	3½" x 42"	4	3½" x 6½"
			4	3½" squares"
Fabric F *Medallion Flower Dk Purple* ⅛ yard	1	2½" x 42"	4	2½" x 4½"
			8	2½" squares

Friendship Flowers Wall Quilt continued	FIRST CUT		SECOND CUT	
	Number of Strips or Pieces	Dimensions	Number of Pieces	Dimensions
BORDERS				
Fabric G *Green Accent Border* ½ yard	2	2½" x 42"	4	2½" x 6½"
			4	2½" x 4½"
	5	1½" x 42" *(for strip piecing)*		
	1	1½" x 42"	8	1½" squares
Fabric H *Purple Accent Border* ¼ yard	4	1¼" x 42"	2	1¼" x 24½"
			2	1¼" x 23"
Fabric I *Border Corner Flowers* ⅙ yard each of two fabrics	1*	3½" x 42" *Cut for each fabric*	8*	3½" squares
Fabric J *Yellow Border Flower & Corner Flower Centers* ⅓ yard	2	3½" x 42"	16	3½" squares
	1	1½" x 42"	16	1½" squares
Fabric K *Border Flower Centers* ⅛ yard	1	1½" x 42"	16	1½" squares
Fabric L *Blue Borders* ⅔ yard	5	2½" x 42" *(for strip piecing)*		
	5	1½" x 42"	4	1½" x 8½"
			12	1½" x 6½"
			40	1½" squares
Binding ½ yard	5	2¾" x 42"		

Backing - 2⅝ yards
Batting - 47" x 47"

GETTING STARTED

This quilt features a 24½" (unfinished) framed center block surrounded by a pieced border. The border includes a total of eight 6½" (unfinished) flower blocks in three different fabric combinations, and eight sashing units: four 9½" long (unfinished) and four 10½" long (unfinished). Refer to Accurate Seam Allowance on page 108. Whenever possible, use the Assembly Line Method on page 108. Press seams in direction of arrows.

Note: We embroidered a floral motif in the center of each sashing unit, stitching the design four times on each of two 15" x 42" Fabric A strips before cutting them into the required segments. We used a Bernina® artista 200E sewing and embroidery system, Bernina artista CD, The Good Life by Debbie Mumm®, design number 47 which we altered with the aid of Bernina artista software. We embroidered eight with four reversed. If you prefer, leave the borders plain, or substitute a fabric with a floral motif to suggest the embroidered design.

MEDALLION FLOWER BLOCK

1. Refer to Quick Corner Triangles on page 108. Sew two 1½" Fabric D squares on opposite corners and one 1½" Fabric C square to one 3½" Fabric B square as shown. Press. Make four.

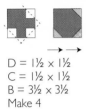

D = 1½ x 1½
C = 1½ x 1½
B = 3½ x 3½
Make 4

2. Sew two units from step 1 together as shown. Press. Make two. Sew these two units together as shown. Press.

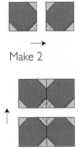

Make 2

3. Making quick corner triangle units, sew one 1½" Fabric D square and one 2½" Fabric F square to one 3½" Fabric E square as shown. Press. Make four, two of each variation.

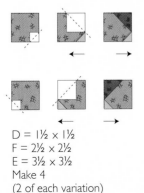

D = 1½ x 1½
F = 2½ x 2½
E = 3½ x 3½
Make 4
(2 of each variation)

4. Sew units from step 3 together in pairs as shown. Press. Make two.

Make 2

5. Sew unit from step 2 between two units from step 4 as shown. Press.

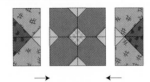

6. Making quick corner triangle units, sew one 1½" Fabric D square and one 2½" Fabric F square to one 3½" x 6½" Fabric E piece as shown. Press. Make four, two of each variation.

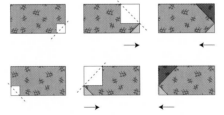

D = 1½ x 1½
F = 2½ x 2½
E = 3½ x 6½
Make 4
(2 of each variation)

7. Sew units from step 6 together in pairs as shown. Press. Make two.

Make 2

8. Sew unit from step 5 between two units from step 7 as shown. Press.

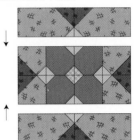

9. Making quick corner triangle units, sew two 2½" Fabric A squares to one 2½" x 4½" Fabric F piece as shown. Press. Make four.

A = 2½ x 2½
F = 2½ x 4½
Make 4

10. Making a quick corner triangle unit, sew one 2½" Fabric A square to one 2½" x 4½" Fabric G piece as shown. Press. Make four, two of each variation.

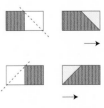

A = 2½ x 2½
G = 2½ x 4½
Make 4
(2 of each variation)

11. Sew one unit from step 9 between one of each unit from step 10 as shown. Press. Make two.

Make 2

12. Making a quick corner triangle unit, sew one 2½" Fabric A square to one 2½" x 6½" Fabric G piece as shown. Press. Make four, two of each variation.

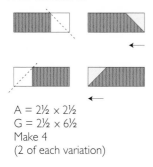

A = 2½ x 2½
G = 2½ x 6½
Make 4
(2 of each variation)

13. Sew one unit from step 9 between one of each unit from step 12 as shown. Press. Make two.

Make 2

14. Sew units from step 11 to top and bottom of unit from step 8 as shown. Press. Sew units from step 13 to sides. Press. Block measures 16½" square.

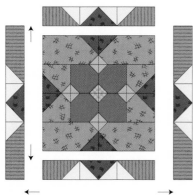

Medallion Flower Block measures 16½" square

15. Sew Fabric A triangles to opposite sides of unit from step 14 as shown. (*Note:* Triangle will extend past edges of square.) Press. Sew triangles to remaining sides. Press. Square unit to 23".

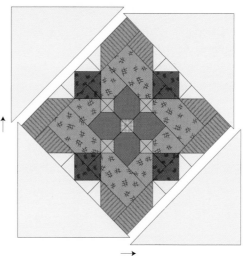

Square unit to 23" square

16. Sew 1¼" x 23" Fabric H strips to top and bottom of unit from step 15. Press seams toward strips. Sew 1¼" x 24½" Fabric H strips to sides. Press.

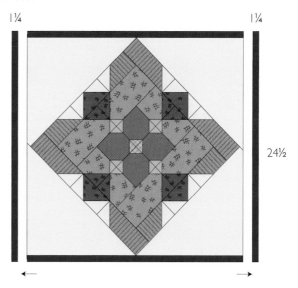

1¼

1¼

24½

BORDERS

1. Refer to Quick Corner Triangles on page 108. Sew one 1½" Fabric A square, one 1½" Fabric K square, and one 1½" Fabric L square to one 3½" Fabric J square as shown. Press. Make sixteen, eight of each variation.

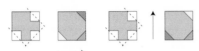

A = 1½ x 1½
K = 1½ x 1½
L = 1½ x 1½
J = 3½ x 3½
Make 16
(8 of each variation)

2. Sew one of each unit from step 1 together as shown. Press. Make eight. Sew two units together as shown. Press. Make four.

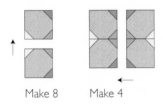

Make 8   Make 4

3. Sew one unit from step 2 between two 1½" x 6½" Fabric L pieces as shown. Press. Make four.

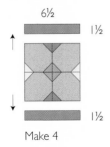

6½
1½
1½
Make 4

4. Sew one 2½" x 42" Fabric L strip and one 1½" x 42" Fabric G strip together as shown. Press. Make five strip sets. Cut into eight 10½" segments and eight 9½" segments as shown.

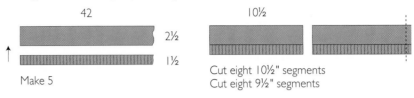

42
2½
1½
Make 5

10½
Cut eight 10½" segments
Cut eight 9½" segments

5. Sew one embroidered 2½" x 9½" Fabric A strip between two 9½" segments from step 4 noting position of embroidery as shown. Make four. Press, repressing seams as shown to make two of each unit.

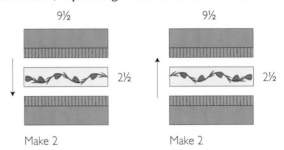

9½   9½
2½   2½

Make 2   Make 2

6. Sew one unit from step 3 between one of each unit from step 5 to make top and bottom border units. Press. Make two. Noting position of embroidery and referring to photo on page 26 and layout on page 32, sew Center Medallion Unit between these two units. Press seams towards borders.

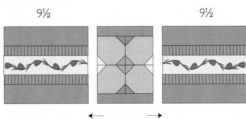

9½   9½

Make 2
Sew Center Medallion Unit between these two units

7. Sew one embroidered 2½" x 10½" Fabric A strip between two 10½" segments from step 4 as shown. Make four. Press, repressing seams as shown to make two of each unit.

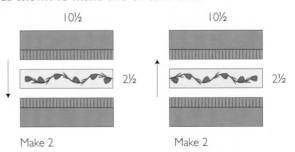

10½   10½
2½   2½

Make 2   Make 2

8. Making quick corner triangle units, sew two 1½" Fabric L squares on opposite corners and one 1½" Fabric J square to one 3½" Fabric I square as shown. Press. Make four, two of each combination.

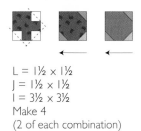

L = 1½ x 1½
J = 1½ x 1½
I = 3½ x 3½
Make 4
(2 of each combination)

9. Making quick corner triangle units, sew one 1½" Fabric L square, one 1½" Fabric J square, and one 1½" Fabric A square to one 3½" Fabric I square as shown. Press. Make eight, two of each variation.

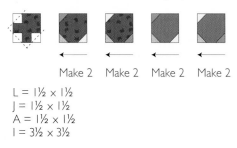

Make 2   Make 2   Make 2   Make 2

L = 1½ x 1½
J = 1½ x 1½
A = 1½ x 1½
I = 3½ x 3½

10. Making quick corner triangle units, sew one 1½" Fabric J square and two 1½" Fabric A squares to one 3½" Fabric I square as shown. Press. Make four, two of each combination.

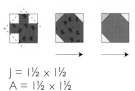

J = 1½ x 1½
A = 1½ x 1½
I = 3½ x 3½
Make 4
(2 of each combination)

11. Arrange and sew one unit from step 8, two units from step 9, and one unit from step 10 together as shown. Press. Make four, two of each combination.

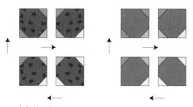

Make 4
(2 of each combination)

12. Sew two 1½" Fabric L squares, two 1½" Fabric G squares, and one 1½" x 2½" Fabric A piece together as shown. Press. Make four.

1½ 1½ 2½ 1½ 1½

▢ ▢ ▢ ▢ ▢ 1½

Make 4

13. Sew one unit from step 11 between one 1½" x 6½" Fabric L piece and one unit from step 12 as shown. Press. Make four, two of each variation noting position of flower unit.

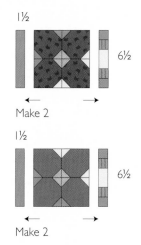

14. Noting position of embroidery and referring to photo on page 26, sew two 1½" x 8½" Fabric L pieces, one of each unit from step 13, and one of each unit from step 7 and one unit from step 3 together. Press. Make two.

15. Referring to photo on page 28 and layout, sew units from step 14 to sides of unit from step 6. Press.

LAYERING & FINISHING

1. Cut backing in half crosswise. Sew pieces together to make one 47" x 80" (approximate) backing piece. Press and trim to 47" x 47". Arrange and baste backing, batting, and top together, referring to Layering the Quilt on page 110.

2. Hand or machine quilt as desired.

3. Sew 2¾" x 42" binding strips end-to-end to make one continuous 2¾"-wide strip. Refer to Binding the Quilt on page 111 and bind quilt to finish.

FRiENDSHiP FLOWERS WALL QUiLT
Finished size: 41" x 41"
Photo: page 28

Friendship Flowers Lap Quilt

This quilt is based on the Medallion Block from Friendship Flowers Wall Quilt and features nine 16½" square blocks (unfinished) and three borders.

Center Medallion Lap Quilt 62" x 62"	FIRST CUT		SECOND CUT	
	Number of Strips or Pieces	Dimensions	Number of Pieces	Dimensions
Fabric A Tan Accent ¾ yard	9	2½" x 42"	144	2½" squares
Fabric B Med Purple ½ yard	4	3½" x 42"	36	3½" squares
Fabric C Orange Centers ⅛ yard	2	1½" x 42"	36	1½" squares
Fabric D Gold Accent ⅓ yard	6	1½" x 42"	144	1½" squares
Fabric E Light Purple 1⅛ yards	10	3½" x 42"	36 / 36	3½" x 6½" / 3½" squares"
Fabric F Dark Purple ⅞ yard	10	2½" x 42"	36 / 72	2½" x 4½" / 2½" squares
Fabric G Green Accent ⅞ yard	11	2½" x 42"	36 / 36	2½" x 6½" / 2½" x 4½"
BORDERS				
First Border ⅓ yard	5	1½" x 42"		
Second Border ½ yard	6	2½" x 42"		
Outside Border ¾ yard	6	4" x 42"		
Binding ⅝ yard	7	2¾" x 42"		
Backing - 3⅞ yards		Batting - 69" x 69"		

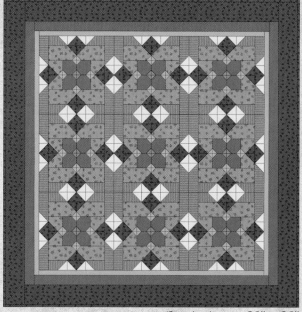

Finished size: 62" x 62"

MAKING THE BLOCKS

Follow steps 1–14 on pages 30-31 for the Medallion Flower Block, making the following quantities:

Step 1–Make thirty-six.
Step 2–Make eighteen, then sew in pairs to make nine.
Step 3–Make thirty-six units, eighteen of each variation.
Step 4–Sew units from step 3 in pairs to make eighteen.
Step 5–Make nine.
Step 6–Make thirty-six units, eighteen of each variation.
Step 7–Make eighteen.
Step 8–Make nine.
Step 9–Make thirty-six.
Step 10–Make thirty-six units, eighteen of each variation.
Step 11–Make eighteen.
Step 12–Make thirty-six units, eighteen of each variation.
Step 13–Make eighteen.
Step 14–Make nine blocks. Blocks measure 16½" square.

ASSEMBLY & FINISHING

1. Referring to layout, arrange and sew blocks in three horizontal rows of three blocks each. Press seams in opposite directions from row to row. Sew rows together. Press.

2. Sew 1½" x 42" First Border Strips end-to-end to make one continuous 1½"- wide strip. Press. Refer to Adding the Borders on page 110 to add border. Repeat for other borders.

3. Cut backing crosswise into two equal pieces. Sew pieces together to make one 69" x 80" (approximate) backing piece. Press and trim to 69" x 69".

4. Baste backing, batting, and top together, referring to Layering the Quilt on page 110. Hand or machine quilt as desired. Sew 2¾" x 42" binding strips end-to-end to make one continuous 2¾"-wide strip. Refer to Binding the Quilt on page 111 and bind quilt to finish.

35

SORBET LAP QUILT

56½" x 70½" • Lap Quilt

This clever confection of a quilt would be a huge hit with any recipient, but the yummy color scheme makes it absolute perfection for your favorite young lady. Not all is sweetness, however! Directional fabric, cut and pieced for dramatic effect, adds a touch of spice.

FABRIC REQUIREMENTS & CUTTING INSTRUCTIONS

Read all instructions before beginning and use ¼"-wide seam allowances throughout. Read Cutting Strips and Pieces on page 108 prior to cutting fabrics.

Sorbet Lap Quilt 56½" x 70½"	FIRST CUT		SECOND CUT	
	Number of Strips or Pieces	Dimensions	Number of Pieces	Dimensions
Fabric A *Background* 2⅛ yards	3	5½" x 42"	2	5½" x 4½"
			44	5½" x 2½"
	3	4½" x 42"	16	4½" x 3½"
			20	4½" x 1½"
	2	3½" x 42" *(for strip piecing)*		
	3	2½" x 42" *(for strip piecing)*		
	11	2½" x 42"	8	2½" x 3½"
			160	2½" squares
Fabric B *Dark Pink* ⅓ yard	2	4½" x 42"	12	4½" squares
Fabric C *Medium Pink* ⅓ yard	2	4½" x 42"	12	4½" squares
Fabric D *Dark Purple* ⅙ yard	1	4½" x 42"	6	4½" squares
			4	4½" x 2½"
Fabric E *Medium Purple* ⅙ yard	1	4½" x 42"	6	4½" squares
			4	4½" x 2½"
Fabric F *Sorbet Stripe* ⅔ yard	4	5½" x 42"	24	5½" "fussy cut" squares
Fabric G *Four-Patch Light* ⅙ yard	1	4½" x 42" *(for strip piecing)*		
Fabric H *Four-Patch & Chain Medium* ⅓ yard	1	4½" x 42" *(for strip piecing)*		
	1	4½" x 42"	3	4½" squares
			6	4½" x 2½"
Fabric I *Chain Light* ⅓ yard	3	3½" x 42" *(for strip piecing)*		
Fabric J *Chain Dark* ¼ yard	2	2½" x 42" *(for strip piecing)*		

Sorbet Lap Quilt continued	FIRST CUT		SECOND CUT	
	Number of Strips or Pieces	Dimensions	Number of Pieces	Dimensions
BORDERS				
First Border ¼ yard	6	1" x 42"		
Second Border ⅓ yard	6	1½" x 42"		
Third Border ⅜ yard	6	2" x 42"		
Outside Border ¾ yard	7	3¼" x 42"		
Binding ⅝ yard	7	2¾" x 42"		

Backing - 3½ yards
Batting - 63" x 77"

GETTING STARTED

This quilt is constructed in units and rows rather than in blocks. Some of the squares are cut from striped fabric (Fabric F) and quick-pieced into quarter-square triangle units for simple—but dramatic—kaleidoscope effects. Depending upon the fabric you choose, you may need to fussy cut the squares so the stripes match up. [*Note:* To make symmetrically striped quarter-square triangle units, four squares must be cut identically.] If you prefer, you can substitute a 4½" fussy-cut square for this pieced unit.

Our method for piecing the quarter-square triangle units yields twelve bonus squares. You won't need them for this quilt; so set them aside for another project such as the Summer Sun Tote Bag on page 96.

Refer to Accurate Seam Allowance on page 108. Whenever possible, use the Assembly Line Method on page 108. Press seams in direction of arrows.

ASSEMBLY

1. Draw a diagonal line on wrong side of one 5½" Fabric F square. Place marked Fabric F square right sides together with another 5½" Fabric F square, making sure colors match and stripes run in same direction. Sew a scant ¼" away from drawn line on both sides to make half-square triangles. Make twelve, drawing line in same direction on each square. Cut on drawn line. Press seams open. This will make twenty-four half-square triangles.

F = 5½ × 5½
Make 12

Make 24

2. Draw a diagonal line on wrong side of twelve units from step 1. Place marked unit right sides together with unmarked unit from step 1, matching seams. Prior to sewing, flip unit to see that stripes are matching. Sew a scant ¼" away from drawn line on both sides. Make twelve. Cut on drawn lines. Press seams open. Square to 4½". This will make twenty-four quarter-square triangles, twelve of each variation as shown. Refer to diagram, to select correct squares for the project. Trim **four** of these squares to 2½" x 4½".

Make 12   Make 24   (Set aside for another project)

Square to 4½
Make 12   Trim 4 to 2½ x 4½   Make 12

3. Refer to Quick Corner Triangles on page 108. Sew four 2½" Fabric A squares to one 4½" Fabric B square as shown. Press. Make twelve and label Unit 1. Sew four 2½" Fabric A squares to one 4½" Fabric C square. Press. Make twelve and label Unit 2. Sew four 2½" Fabric A squares to one 4½" Fabric D square. Press. Make six and label Unit 3. Sew four 2½" Fabric A squares to one 4½" Fabric E square. Press. Make six and label Unit 4.

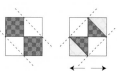   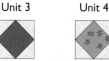

Unit 1   Unit 2   Unit 3   Unit 4

A = 2½ × 2½
B = 4½ × 4½
Make 12

A = 2½ × 2½
C = 4½ × 4½
Make 12

A = 2½ × 2½
D = 4½ × 4½
Make 6

A = 2½ × 2½
E = 4½ × 4½
Make 6

4. Sew one 4½" x 1½" Fabric A piece to one Unit 1 from step 3 as shown. Press. Make six. Repeat to make six of unit 2, taking care to orient stripe as shown. Make four of each using Units 3 and 4.

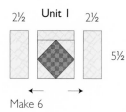

Unit 1

4½
1½

Unit 2   Unit 3   Unit 4

Make 6   Make 6   Make 4   Make 4

5. Sew each unit from step 4 between two 5½" x 2½" Fabric A pieces as shown. Press. Make six of each using Units 1 and 2, and four of each using Units 3 and 4.

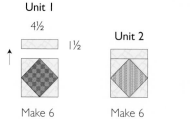

2½   Unit 1   2½

5½

Unit 2   Unit 3   Unit 4

Make 6   Make 6   Make 4   Make 4

6. Sew one 3½" x 42" Fabric A strip and one 2½" x 42" Fabric J strip together to make a strip set as shown. Press. Make two strips sets. Cut strip sets into twenty-four 2½"-wide segments.

 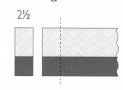

42   2½

3½
2½

Make 2   Cut 24 segments

7. Sew one 3½" x 42" Fabric I strip and one 2½" x 42" Fabric A strip together to make a strip set as shown. Press. Make three strip sets. Cut strip sets into twenty-four 3½"-wide segments. Sew segments from steps 6 and 7 together as shown. Press. Make twenty-four.

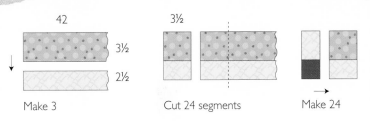

Make 3   Cut 24 segments   Make 24

8. Arrange and sew two 5½" x 2½" Fabric A pieces, four units from step 7, one Unit 1 from step 5, one Unit 2 from step 5, and one 5½" x 4½" Fabric A piece noting position of units as shown. Press. Label Row A.

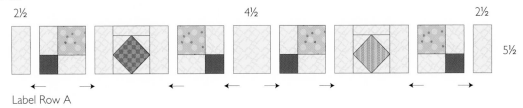

Label Row A

9. Repeat step 8, turning each unit as shown. Press. Label Row E.

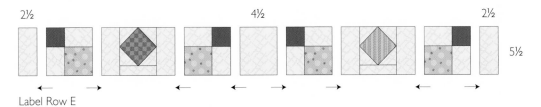

Label Row E

10. Sew one 4½" x 3½" Fabric A piece to each remaining unit from step 3 as shown. Press. Make six of each using Units 1 and 2, taking care to orient stripe in Unit 2 as shown. Make two of each using Units 3 and 4.

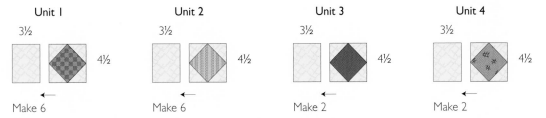

Unit I   Unit 2   Unit 3   Unit 4
Make 6   Make 6   Make 2   Make 2

11. Arrange and sew two 4½" x 2½" Fabric H pieces, two of Unit 1 from step 10, two of Unit 2 from step 10, two quarter-square units from step 2, and one 4½" Fabric H square as shown. Press. Make three and label Row B.

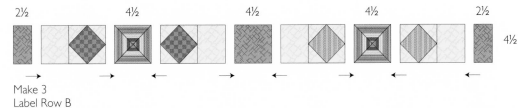

Make 3
Label Row B

39

12. Make quick corner triangle units. Sew two 2½" Fabric A squares to one 4½" x 2½" Fabric D piece as shown. Press. Make four. Sew two 2½" Fabric A squares to one 4½" x 2½" Fabric E piece. Press. Make four.

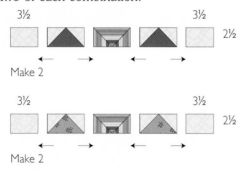

A = 2½ x 2½
D = 4½ x 2½
Make 4

A = 2½ x 2½
E = 4½ x 2½
Make 4

13. Arrange and sew two 2½" x 3½" Fabric A pieces, two matching units from step 12, and one 2½" x 4½" unit from step 2 as shown. Press. Make two of each combination.

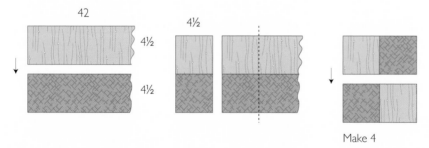

3½   3½   2½
Make 2

3½   3½   2½
Make 2

14. Sew 4½" x 42" Fabric G strip to 4½" x 42" Fabric H strip as shown. Press. Cut strip set into eight 4½"-wide segments. Sew units together in pairs as shown. Press. Make four.

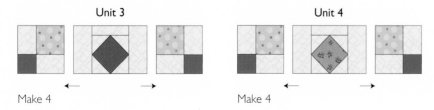

42
4½
4½

4½

Make 4

15. Sew one Unit 3 from step 5 between two units from step 7 noting position of unit 3 as shown. Press. Make four. Sew one Unit 4 from step 5 between two units from step 7. Press. Make four.

Unit 3   Unit 4

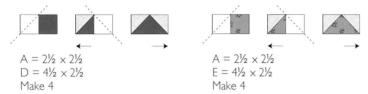

Make 4   Make 4

16. Sew unit from step 14 between Units 1 and 2 from step 5 as shown noting position of Units 1 and 2. Press. Make four.

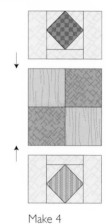

Make 4

17. Sew 4½" square unit from step 2 between two matching units from step 10 as shown. Press. Make two, one of each combination.

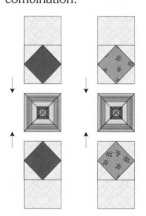

Make 2
(1 of each combination)

18. Arrange and sew two matching units from step 13, two of Unit 3 from step 15, two units from step 16, two of Unit 4 from step 15, and one unit from step 17 as shown. Press. Label Row C.

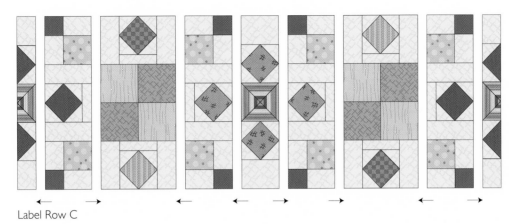

Label Row C

19. Arrange and sew two matching units from step 13, two of Unit 4 from step 15, two units from step 16, two of Unit 3 from step 15, and one unit from step 17 as shown. Label Row D.

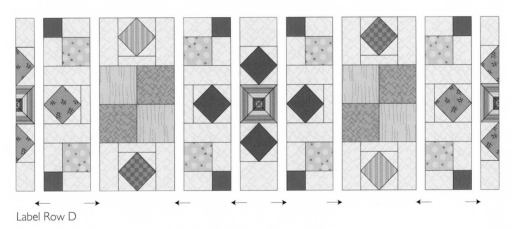

Label Row D

20. Referring to photo on page 36 and layout on page 42, arrange Rows A, B, C, B, D, B, and E. Sew rows together. Press.

BORDERS

1. Sew 1" x 42" First Border strips end-to-end to make one continuous 1"-wide strip. Press. Refer to Adding the Borders on page 110. Measure the quilt through center from side to side. Cut two 1"-wide First Border strips to that measurement. Sew to top and bottom of quilt. Press seams toward border.

2. Measure quilt through center from top to bottom, including borders just added. Cut two 1"-wide First Border strips to that measurement. Sew to sides of quilt. Press.

3. Refer to steps 1 and 2 to join, measure, trim, and sew 1½"-wide Second Border strips, 2"-wide Third Border strips, and 3¼"-wide Outside Border strips to top, bottom, and sides of quilt. Press seams toward each newly added border strip.

LAYERING & FINISHING

1. Cut backing crosswise into two equal pieces. Sew pieces together to make one 63" x 80" (approximate) backing piece. Press.

2. Arrange and baste backing, batting, and top together, referring to Layering the Quilt on page 110.

3. Hand or machine quilt as desired.

4. Sew 2¾" x 42" binding strips end-to-end to make one continuous 2¾"-wide strip. Refer to Binding the Quilt on page 111 and bind quilt to finish.

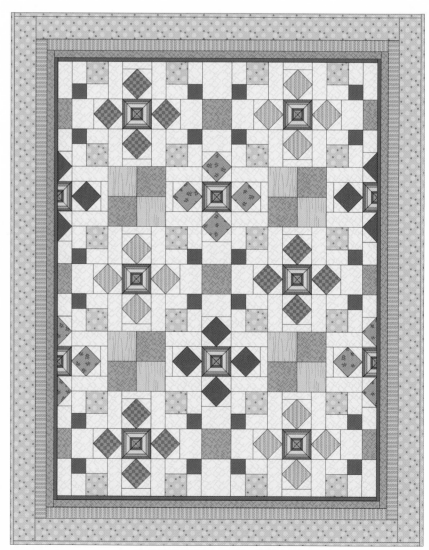

SORBET LAP QUILT
Finished size: 56½" x 70½"
Photo: page 36

Memory Maker Message Board

Featuring the same sweet colors as the Sorbet Lap Quilt, this message board made with polka dot & checked ribbons & a variety of bright buttons will organize and add a cheerful accent to any room.

MATERIALS NEEDED

¼" Foam Core - 20" x 26" piece
Batting - 26" x 32" piece
Background Fabric - ⅞ yard
  28" x 34" piece
¾"-wide Checked Ribbon - 4⅛ yards
¾"-wide Polka Dot Ribbon - 4⅛ yards
Standard Paper Stapler
Long Needle and Embroidery Floss
See-Through Ruler with 45° Angle
Buttons - 17 Assorted
Picture-Hanging Wire - 8" piece
Low Temperature Glue Gun

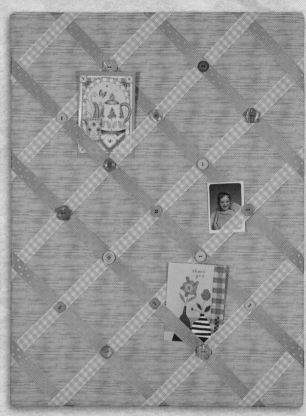

Finished size: 20" x 26"

MAKING THE BULLETIN BOARD

Note: We chose foam core for this project because it is lightweight to hang and a needle will go through it. A standard office stapler that will open flat is recommended for this project. A staple gun may dent the lightweight foam core.

1. To position a wire for hanging, measure down 3" from top of foam core and mark spot in center. Mark a spot 1½" on each side of first mark. Punch small holes at outside points and thread 8" long picture-hanging wire through holes. Knot and twist ends of wire together to form a hanger for message board.

2. Lay batting over foam core piece. Then place 28" x 34" Background Fabric over batting. Turn to back side and gently pull fabric to the back on one side and use a standard stapler to fasten, stopping at corners. Repeat for opposite side, then stretch and staple fabric at top and bottom, stopping at corners. Trim excess batting from corners so batting does not overlap, then pull corner fabric tight and check front to make sure there are no ruffles in fabric. Staple corner fabric in back.

3. Cut one piece of each ribbon to 33". For each ribbon, cut the following lengths twice: 28", 19", and 10".

4. Referring to photo and using ruler, lay ribbon on message board at 45° angles. Center of each corner ribbon is approximately 4" from the corner. Position corner ribbons then arrange ribbons equidistant from each other on the message board. Turn ends of each ribbon to the back and temporarily fasten with removable tape. After ribbons are arranged as desired, weave ribbons at intersections so the ribbon on top alternates. Staple ends of ribbons in the back to fasten, and remove tape.

5. Referring to photo, arrange buttons at intersections. Using needle and six strands of embroidery floss, pull thread through **every other** button and all layers including the foam core, tying ends of the thread in the back of foam core to affix buttons to message board. Use a low temperature glue gun to affix remaining buttons to top ribbon only. Cards and photos will tuck in behind the ribbons. Use the wire hanger to hang message board.

43

KiCK UP YOUR HEELS

36" x 33" • Wall Quilt

Quick-fuse appliqué, digitized embroidery, a dynamite new product called pet screen…and shoes!
This very chic, very versatile wall piece—complete with cunning catch-all pocket—seems to have it all.
It's equally at home storing accessories, notions, or whatnots in any room of your home.

FABRIC REQUIREMENTS & CUTTING INSTRUCTIONS

Read all instructions before beginning and use ¼"-wide seam allowances throughout. Read Cutting Strips and Pieces on page 108 prior to cutting fabrics.

Kick Up Your Heels Wall Quilt 36" x 33"	FIRST CUT		SECOND CUT	
	Number of Strips or Pieces	Dimensions	Number of Pieces	Dimensions
Fabric A *Background* ¾ yard	1	24½" × 27½"		
Fabric B *Pet Screen* ⅜ yard	1	9½" × 36" *Trimmed to 5" x 27" after embroidering*		
	1	1" × 27"		
	3	1" × 18½"		
	2	1" × 12"		
BORDERS				
First Border ⅙ yard	4	1" × 42"	2	1" × 27½"
			2	1" × 25½"
Second Border ⅙ yard	4	1" × 42"	2	1" × 28½"
			2	1" × 26½"
Third Border & Pocket Trim ⅓ yard	1	2½" × 42" (pocket trim)	2	1½" × 29½"
	4	1½" × 42"	2	1½" × 28½"
Fourth Border ⅙ yard	4	1" × 42"	2	1" × 31½"
			2	1" × 29½"
Outside Border ⅓ yard	4	2" × 42"	4	2" × 32½" "fussy cut"
Binding ⅝ yard for bias OR ⅜ yard	4	2¾" bias strips cut from a 21" square OR		
	4	2¾" × 42"		

Backing - 1⅛ yards
Batting - 40" × 37"
Boot Appliqué - ⅓ yard or fat quarter
Pump Appliqué - ¼ yard or fat quarter
Assorted Shoe Appliqués - Assorted Scraps
Assorted Shoe Trims
Embroidery Thread - Green & two golds
Lightweight Fusible Web - ½ yard
Stabilizer - 1 yard

GETTING STARTED

This quilt features a single block divided to showcase four different shoe appliqués. Rather than traditional sashing, we used decorative machine stitches to sew strips of pet screen to the background to frame each appliqué. We finished the quilt with an embroidered pocket—also cut from pet screen—and a series of simple borders. Using Bernina Embroidery Software and a Bernina Artista 200E, the Flower pattern on page 47 was digitized and embroidered on the pet screen prior to cutting for the pocket. Note that we fussy cut the Outside Border in order to match the plaid.

Pet screen is a versatile nylon screen that you can cut with rotary cutter or scissors. Ask for it at your local quilt shop. Although it can be pressed lightly using a pressing cloth and a dry iron set at moderate temperature, we preferred to add the screen after the quilt was quilted to avoid potential problems with the screen melting. (We also found the screen easier to attach when stitched through all three layers of the quilt.) Since quilting can sometimes cause the quilt to "shrink" a bit, we recommend you remeasure and trim the screen strips as needed before sewing them to the quilt.

Refer to Accurate Seam Allowance on page 108. Whenever possible, use the Assembly Line Method on page 108. Press seams in direction of arrows.

MAKING THE QUILT TOP

1. Refer to Adding the Borders on page 110. Sew 1" x 27½" First Border strips to top and bottom of 24½" x 27½" Fabric A piece. Press seams toward border. Sew 1" x 25½" First Border strips to sides. Press.

2. Refer to step 1 to sew 1" x 28½" Second Border strips to top and bottom and 1" x 26½" Second Border strips to sides. Press. Sew 1½" x 29½" Third Border strips to top and bottom and 1½" x 28½" Third Border strips to sides. Press. Sew 1" x 31½" Fourth Border strips to top and bottom and 1" x 29½" Fourth Border strips to sides. Press. Sew 2" x 32½" Outside Border strips to top, bottom, then sides of quilt. Press.

ADDING THE APPLIQUÉS

Refer to appliqué instructions on page 109. Our instructions are for Quick-Fuse Appliqué, but if you prefer hand appliqué, reverse patterns and add ¼"-wide seam allowances.

1. Use patterns on pages 47 and 48 to make templates for loafer (3 pieces), slide (3 pieces), and pump (1 piece). Refer to diagram and instructions on page 47 to make template for boot (2 pieces). Use shoe fabrics and assorted scraps to cut one of each appliqué piece.

2. Refer to diagram below. Use a removable marker to mark positions for pet screen on Fabric A as shown. This will provide guidelines for centering appliqués.

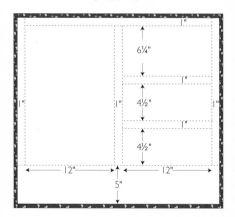

3. Refer to photo on page 44 and layout to position appliqués on marked background. Fuse appliqués and finish with machine satin stitch or other decorative stitching as desired.

LAYERING & FINISHING

1. Arrange and baste backing, batting, and top together, referring to Layering the Quilt on page 110. Hand or machine quilt as desired.

2. Remeasure and trim the pet screen strips as needed before sewing them to the quilt. Referring to photo on page 44, layout, and diagram at left, position and stitch 1"-wide strips of pet screen to the quilt. We stitched down the center of each strip using stitch #138 on the Bernina® artista 200E and 12-weight green cotton embroidery thread. The screen doesn't ravel so there is no need to finish the edges.

3. Using embroidery software, digitize flower pattern on page 47. Use a fill stitch for petals and center and an outline stitch for petal accents and outline.

4. Embroider flower (pattern on page 47) in center of 9½" x 36" strip of pet screen using two gold and one green embroidery threads. Embroider two flowers on each side of center flower, spacing them so flower centers are 5" apart. Trim screen to 5" x 27". Place screen on quilt front and trim to fit if needed. (Ours measures 5" x 26½".) Optional: Use crewel yarn to embroider flowers.

KiCK UP YOUR HEELS WALL QUiLT

Finished size: *36" x 33"*
Photo: *page 44*

Kick Up Your Heels Wall Quilt Patterns

Patterns are reversed for use with Quick-Fuse Appliqué (page 109).

Tracing Line ——————
Tracing Line - - - - - - -
(will be hidden behind other fabrics)
Extension Line — · — · — ·

For Boot, draw an extension line through and beyond pattern extension lines to make boot 16¼" tall from sole. Top is 6½" wide.

16¼

6½

For pump trace a reverse of solid outside lines to make one solid piece.

Boot & Pump

5. Fold and press 2½" x 42" Pocket Trim strip in half lengthwise with wrong sides together. Trim to 28". Referring to Binding the Quilt on page 111, pin and sew folded strip to wrong side of top edge of trimmed screen, allowing strip to overlap ends by ½". Turn under ends of folded strip, turn strip to front of screen, and stitch in place.

6. Referring to photo on page 44 and layout, position screen on quilt. Use invisible thread and double row of stitching to secure screen to quilt along side and bottom edges. Stitch between first and second embroidered flower to create pocket. Repeat between fourth and fifth flowers.

7. Refer to Making Bias Strips on page 110. Sew 2¾" x 42" bias binding strips end-to-end to make one continuous 2¾"-wide strip. Refer to Binding the Quilt on page 111 and bind quilt to finish.

8. Referring to photo on page 44 and layout, add decorative shoe trims or other embellishments to shoe appliqués, as desired.

Flower Embroidery Pattern

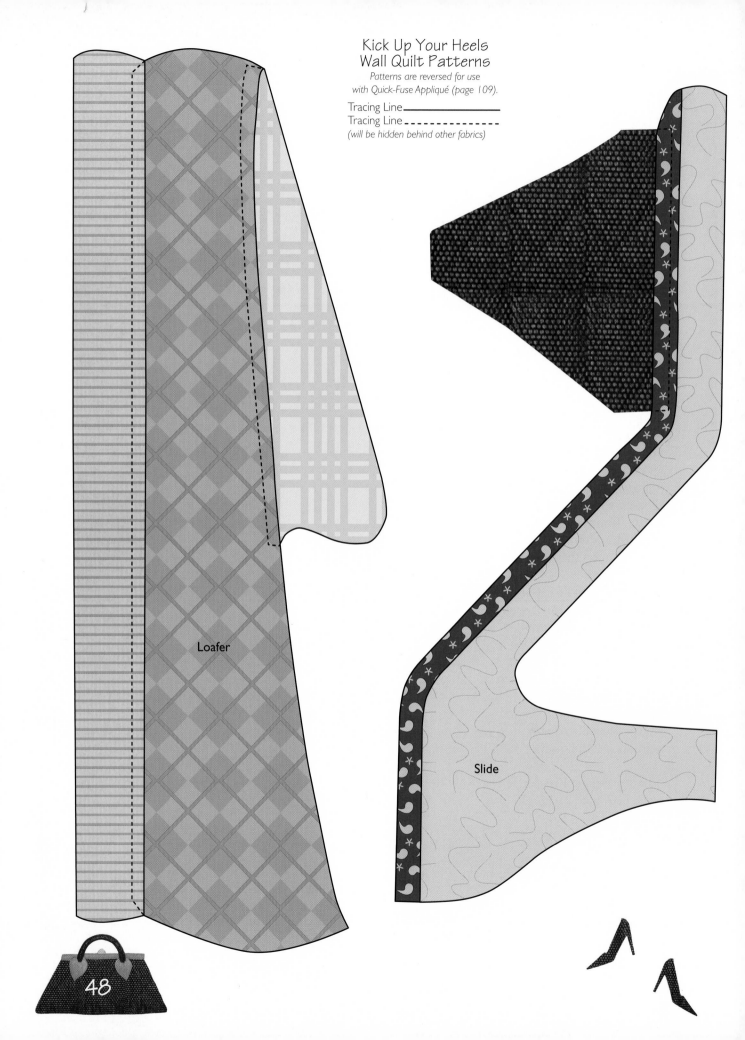

Kick Up Your Heels
Wall Quilt Patterns
*Patterns are reversed for use
with Quick-Fuse Appliqué (page 109).*

Tracing Line————————
Tracing Line------------------
(will be hidden behind other fabrics)

Loafer

Slide

Daisy Days Jewelry Armoire

Bright as a daisy, this fabric-covered jewelry armoire coordinates perfectly with the Kick Up Your Heels Quilt to create a beautiful boudoir. A thrift store find takes on posh appeal with a little fabric and decoupage.

MATERIALS NEEDED

Jewelry Armoire
Mod Podge® in Matte Finish
Assorted Fabrics
Freezer Paper
Black Acrylic Craft Paint
Assorted Paintbrushes

MAKING THE DECOUPAGE ARMOIRE

1. Using our photo and the features of your armoire as inspiration, determine placement of each fabric.

2. If desired, refer to Kick Up Your Heels Wall Quilt, Layering and Finishing on page 46 step 4 to embroider a daisy on a central fabric piece.

3. Use freezer paper to make patterns for each fabric piece marking on dull side of freezer paper. Iron each freezer paper pattern to right side of the selected fabric. Cut out each piece and remove freezer paper.

4. Use black acrylic paint to paint all edges and depressed and raised sections of armoire and allow to dry. This way if fabric pieces don't fit exactly on odd shapes, the black color will hide imperfections.

5. Apply Mod Podge® to one section of armoire and carefully place selected fabric on section, aligning all edges, and smoothing out any wrinkles or bubbles. Allow to dry before using the same procedure for other areas of armoire.

6. When all fabric pieces have been applied, allow to dry then cover entire armoire with one or more coats of Mod Podge®.

This same technique will work for a small chest of drawers, night table, or other furniture piece.

AROUND THE BLOCK

84" x 84" • Quilt

A galaxy of stellar blocks and a nifty pieced setting are the "stars" in this dazzling, bed-sized sampler quilt. With its constellation of colorful fabrics and quick-pieced construction, it's a guaranteed sensation in any quilter's universe.

FABRIC REQUIREMENTS & CUTTING INSTRUCTIONS

Read all instructions before beginning and use ¼"-wide seam allowances throughout. Read Cutting Strips and Pieces on page 108 prior to cutting fabrics.

Around the Block Quilt 84" x 84"	FIRST CUT		SECOND CUT		Around the Block Quilt continued	FIRST CUT		SECOND CUT	
	Number of Strips or Pieces	Dimensions	Number of Pieces	Dimensions		Number of Strips or Pieces	Dimensions	Number of Pieces	Dimensions
Fabric A Background ½ yard	4 2	2½" x 42" 1½" x 42"	12 32 8 8	2½" x 4½" 2½" squares 1½" x 4½" 1½" x 2½"	Fabric M Striped Gold ⅛ yard*	1	4½" x 42"	5 2	4½" x 1½"* 2" x 1½"*
Fabric B Background ⅜ yard	1 3	3" x 42" 2½" x 42"	10 44	3" squares 2½" squares	Fabric N Dark Green ⅜ yard	2 3 1	3" squares 2½" x 42" 1½" x 42"	45 8	2½" squares 1½" squares
Fabric C Background ⅜ yard	4 1	2½" x 42" 1½" x 42"	8 8 12 4 12 4	2½" x 8½" 2½" x 4½" 2½" squares 2" squares 1½" x 2½" 1½" squares	Fabric O Light Green ⅓ yard	1 1 1	4½" x 42" 2½" x 42" 1½" x 42"	4 4 4 8 8	4½" squares 2½" x 4½" 2½" squares 1½" x 2½" 1½" squares
Fabric D Sashing ¾ yard	1 9	4½" x 42" 2" x 42"	1 8 20 20	4½" square 4⅜" squares 2" x 9⅜" 2" x 6⅜"	Fabric P Dark Blue ¼ yard	2 1	2½" x 42" 1½" x 42"	4 24 4	2½" x 4½" 2½" squares 1½" squares
Fabric E Sashing ½ yard	10	1½" x 42"	36 36	1½" x 6⅜" 1½" x 4⅜"	Fabric Q Light Blue ⅓ yard	1 2	4½" x 42" 2½" x 42"	5 4 20 4	4½" squares 2½" x 4½" 2½" squares 1½" squares
Fabric F Sashing ¾ yard	2 7	4⅜" x 42" 2" x 42"	10 16 16	4⅜" squares 2" x 9⅜" 2" x 6⅜"	**BORDERS**				
Fabric G Dark Red ⅔ yard	1 3 3	5" x 42" 3" x 42" 2½" x 42"	4 32 8 20 4	5" squares 3" squares 2½" x 4½" 2½" squares 2" squares	First Border ⅝ yard	6	3" x 42"	12 4	3" x 17½" 3" squares
Fabric H Star Red ⅝ yard	1 3 1	5" x 42" 3" x 42" 2½" x 42"	4 32 8 1 2	5" squares 3" squares 2½" squares 1½" x 4½" 1½" x 2"	Second Border ⅓ yard	6	1½" x 42"		
					Third Border ⅝ yard	7	2½" x 42"		
Fabric I Light Red ⅓ yard	1 1 1	4½" x 42" 2½" x 42" 1½" x 42"	4 4 2 13 8	4½" squares 4½" x 1½" 3" squares 2½" squares 1½" squares	Fourth Border ⅜ yard	7	1½" x 42"		
					Fifth Border ½ yard	7	2" x 42"		
Fabric J Dark Gold ⅓ yard	1 2	4½" x 42" 2½" x 42"	1 8 28	4½" square 3" squares 2½" squares	Sixth Border 1¼ yards	1 8	5" x 42" 4½" x 42"	2	5" squares
Fabric K Light Gold ¼ yard	2	2½" x 42"	4 24	2½" x 4½" 2½" squares	Outside Border 1¼ yards	1 8	5" x 42" 4½" x 42"	6	5" squares
Fabric L Yellow ¼ yard	1 1 1	3" x 42" 2½" x 42" 1½" x 42"	2 12 4 4	3" squares 2½" squares 1½" x 2½" 1½" squares	Binding ¾ yard	9	2¾" x 42"		

Backing - 7¾ yards
Batting - 92" x 92"

For directional fabric, the measurement that is listed first runs parallel to selvage (strip width).

GETTING STARTED

This quilt includes nine 12½" (unfinished) blocks: two Boxed Star Blocks, two Octagonal Star Blocks, two Double Star Blocks, two Pinwheel Star Blocks, and one Center Block. Each of the four star blocks is made in two different fabric combinations, instructions are illustrated in each step with both color variations.

The blocks are turned on point and squared with pieced-triangle sashing, so the overall construction is simple and straightforward.

Refer to Accurate Seam Allowance on page 108. Whenever possible, use the Assembly Line Method on page 108. Press seams in direction of arrows.

BOXED STAR

1. Sew one 2" x 1½" Fabric M piece between two 2" Fabric G squares as shown. Press. Make two and label Block 1. Sew one 1½" x 2" Fabric H piece between two 2" Fabric C squares. Press. Make two and label Block 2.

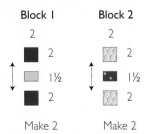

2. Sew one 4½" x 1½" Fabric M piece between two Block 1 units from step 1 as shown. Press. Sew 1½" x 4½" Fabric H piece between two Block 2 units from step 1. Press.

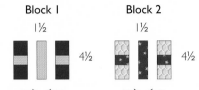

3. Refer to Quick Corner Triangles on page 108. Sew one 2½" Fabric J square and one 2½" Fabric N square to one 2½" x 4½" Fabric A piece as shown. Press. Make twelve and label Block 1. Sew one 2½" Fabric Q square and one 2½" Fabric I square to one 2½" x 4½" Fabric C piece as shown. Press. Make four and label Block 2. Sew one 2½" Fabric N square and one 2½" Fabric Q square to one 2½" x 4½" Fabric C piece. Press. Make four and label Block 2.

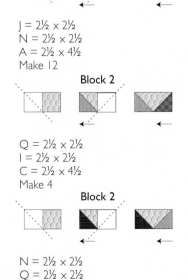

J = 2½ × 2½
N = 2½ × 2½
A = 2½ × 4½
Make 12

Block 2

Q = 2½ × 2½
I = 2½ × 2½
C = 2½ × 4½
Make 4

Block 2

N = 2½ × 2½
Q = 2½ × 2½
C = 2½ × 4½
Make 4

4. Making quick corner triangle units, sew one 2½" Fabric I square and one 2½" Fabric N square to one 2½" x 4½" Fabric O piece as shown. Press. Make four and label Block 2.

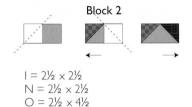

I = 2½ × 2½
N = 2½ × 2½
O = 2½ × 4½
Make 4

5. Making a quick corner triangle unit, sew one 2½" Fabric J square to one 2½" Fabric N square as shown. Press. Make four.

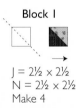

J = 2½ × 2½
N = 2½ × 2½
Make 4

6. Sew two Block 1 units from step 3 together as shown. Press. Make four. Sew one of each Block 2 units from step 3 together as shown. Press. Make four.

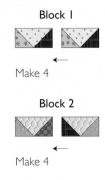

Make 4

Make 4

7. Sew one Block 1 unit from step 3 between two units from step 5 as shown. Press. Make two. Sew one unit from step 4 between two 2½" Fabric Q squares. Press. Make two.

Block 1

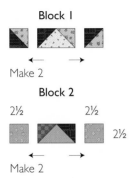

Make 2

Block 2

2½ 2½

2½

Make 2

8. Sew one Block 1 unit from step 2 between two Block 1 units from step 3 as shown. Press. Sew one Block 2 unit from step 2 between two units from step 4 as shown. Press.

Block 1

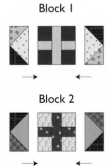

Block 2

9. Sew two Block 1 units from step 6, two Block 1 units from step 7, and Block 1 unit from step 8 together as shown. Press. Repeat using Block 2 units from steps 6, 7, and 8.

Block 1   **Block 2**

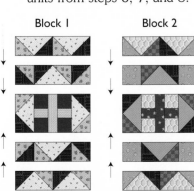

10. Sew one Block 1 unit from step 6 between two 2½" Fabric A squares as shown. Press. Make two. Sew one Block 2 unit from step 6 between two 2½" Fabric C squares. Press. Make two.

Block 1

2½   2½

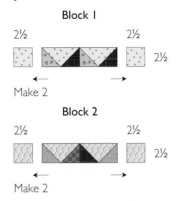

2½

Make 2

Block 2

2½   2½

2½

Make 2

11. Sew Block 1 unit from step 9 between two Block 1 units from step 10 as shown. Press. Repeat using Block 2 units from steps 9 and 10. Blocks measure 12½" square.

Block 1

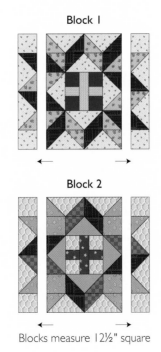

Block 2

Blocks measure 12½" square

OCTAGONAL STAR

1. Refer to Quick Corner Triangles on page 108. Sew four 2½" Fabric P squares to one 4½" Fabric J square as shown. Press and label Block 3. Sew four 2½" Fabric K squares to one 4½" Fabric Q square as shown. Press and label Block 4.

Block 3

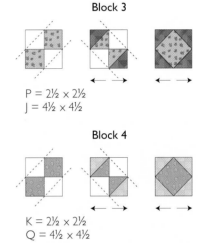

P = 2½ × 2½
J = 4½ × 4½

Block 4

K = 2½ × 2½
Q = 4½ × 4½

2. Making quick corner triangle units, sew two 2½" Fabric L squares to one 2½" x 4½" Fabric G piece as shown. Press. Make four and label Block 3. Sew two 2½" Fabric N squares to one 2½" x 4½" Fabric K piece. Press. Make four and label Block 4.

Block 3

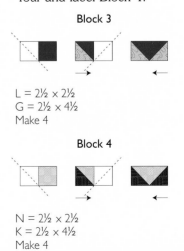

L = 2½ × 2½
G = 2½ × 4½
Make 4

Block 4

N = 2½ × 2½
K = 2½ × 4½
Make 4

3. Sew Block 3 unit from step 1 between two Block 3 units from step 2. Press. Repeat using Block 4 units from steps 1 and 2.

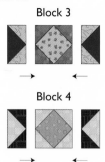

Block 3

Block 4

4. Making a quick corner triangle unit, sew one 2½" Fabric P square to one 2½" Fabric G square as shown. Press. Make four and label Block 3. Sew one 2½" Fabric P square to one 2½" Fabric K square as shown. Press. Make four and label Block 4.

Block 3   **Block 4**

P = 2½ × 2½   P = 2½ × 2½
G = 2½ × 2½   K = 2½ × 2½
Make 4   Make 4

5. Sew one Block 3 unit from step 2 between two Block 3 units from step 4. Press. Make two. Repeat using Block 4 units from steps 2 and 4. Make two.

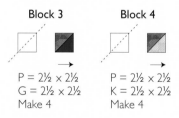

Block 3

Make 2

Block 4

Make 2

6. Making quick corner triangle units, sew two 2½" Fabric B squares to one 2½" x 4½" Fabric Q piece as shown. Press. Make four and label Block 3. Sew two 2½" Fabric A squares to one 2½" x 4½" Fabric P piece as shown. Press. Make four and label Block 4.

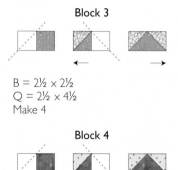

Block 3

B = 2½ × 2½
Q = 2½ × 4½
Make 4

Block 4

A = 2½ × 2½
P = 2½ × 4½
Make 4

7. Making a quick corner triangle unit, sew one 2½" Fabric B square to one 2½" Fabric J square as shown. Press. Make eight and label Block 3. Sew one 2½" Fabric A square to one 2½" Fabric G square as shown. Press. Make eight and label Block 4.

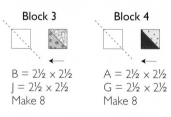

Block 3   **Block 4**

B = 2½ × 2½   A = 2½ × 2½
J = 2½ × 2½   G = 2½ × 2½
Make 8   Make 8

8. Sew one Block 3 unit from step 6 between two Block 3 units from step 7 as shown. Press. Make four. Repeat using Block 4 units from steps 6 and 7. Make four.

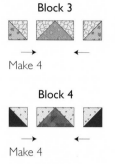

Block 3

Make 4

Block 4

Make 4

9. Sew Block 3 unit from step 3, two Block 3 units from step 5, and two Block 3 units from step 8 together as shown. Press. Repeat using Block 4 units from steps 3, 5, and 8.

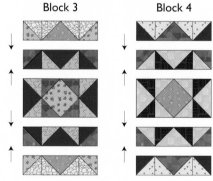

Block 3   **Block 4**

10. Sew one Block 3 unit from step 8 between two 2½" Fabric B squares as shown. Press. Make two. Sew one Block 4 unit from step 8 between two 2½" Fabric A squares. Press. Make two.

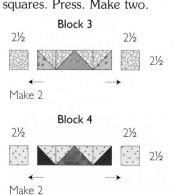

Block 3

2½   2½

2½

Make 2

Block 4

2½   2½

2½

Make 2

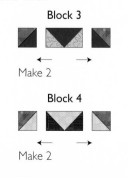

11. Sew Block 3 unit from step 9 between two Block 3 units from step 10. Press. Repeat using Block 4 units from steps 9 and 10. Block measures 12½" square.

Block 3

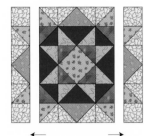

Block 4

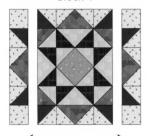

Blocks measure 12½" square

DOUBLE STAR

1. Refer to Quick Corner Triangles on page 108. Sew two 1½" Fabric O squares to one 1½" x 2½" Fabric L piece as shown. Press. Make four and label Block 5. Sew one 1½" Fabric Q square and one 1½" Fabric P square to one 1½" x 2½" Fabric C piece as shown. Press. Make four and label Block 6.

Block 5

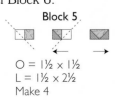

O = 1½ x 1½
L = 1½ x 2½
Make 4

Block 6

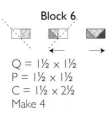

Q = 1½ x 1½
P = 1½ x 1½
C = 1½ x 2½
Make 4

2. Sew one 2½" Fabric I square between two Block 5 units from step 1 as shown. Press. Sew one 2½" Fabric N square between two Block 6 units from step 1. Press.

Block 5   **Block 6**

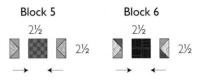

2½   2½   2½   2½

3. Sew one Block 5 unit from step 1 between two 1½" Fabric L squares as shown. Press. Make two. Sew one Block 6 unit from step 1 between two 1½" Fabric C squares. Press. Make two.

Block 5   **Block 6**

1½   1½   1½   1½

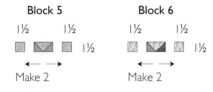

1½   1½

Make 2   Make 2

4. Sew Block 5 unit from step 2 between two Block 5 units from step 3 as shown. Press. Repeat using Block 6 units from steps 2 and 3. Press.

Block 5   **Block 6**

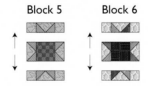

5. Making a quick corner triangle unit, sew one 1½" Fabric N square to one 1½" x 2½" Fabric C piece as shown. Press. Make eight, four of each variation. Sew units together in pairs as shown. Press. Make four and label Block 5. Sew one 1½" Fabric I square to one 1½" x 2½" Fabric O piece as shown. Press. Make eight, four of each variation. Sew units together in pairs as shown. Press. Make four and label Block 6.

Block 5

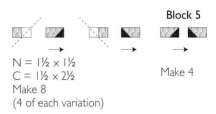

N = 1½ x 1½
C = 1½ x 2½
Make 8
(4 of each variation)

Make 4

Block 6

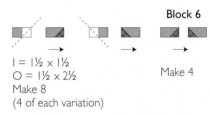

I = 1½ x 1½
O = 1½ x 2½
Make 8
(4 of each variation)

Make 4

6. Sew 4½" x 1½" Fabric I piece to Block 5 unit from step 5 as shown. Press. Make four. Sew 4½" x 1½" Fabric M piece to Block 6 unit from step 5. Press. Make four.

Block 5   **Block 6**

4½   4½

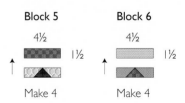

1½   1½

Make 4   Make 4

7. Making a quick corner triangle unit, sew one 2½" Fabric N square to one 2½" Fabric O square as shown. Press. Make four and label Block 5. Sew one 2½" Fabric P square to one 2½" Fabric Q square. Press. Make four and label Block 6.

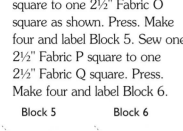

Block 5   Block 6

N = 2½ × 2½   P = 2½ × 2½
O = 2½ × 2½   Q = 2½ × 2½
Make 4   Make 4

8. Sew Block 5 unit from step 6 between two Block 5 units from step 7 as shown. Press. Make two. Repeat using Block 6 units from steps 6 and 7.

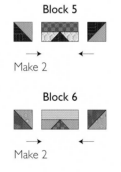

Block 5

Make 2

Block 6

Make 2

9. Arrange and sew Block 5 unit from step 4 between two Block 5 units from step 6 as shown. Press. Sew Block 5 units from step 8 to sides as shown. Repeat using Block 6 units from steps 4, 6, and 8.

Block 5   Block 6

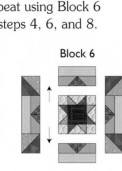

10. Making quick corner triangle units, sew two 2½" Fabric H squares to one 2½" x 8½" Fabric C piece as shown. Press. Make four and label Block 5. Sew one 2½" Fabric Q square and one 2½" Fabric P square to one 2½" x 8½" Fabric C piece. Press. Make four and label Block 6.

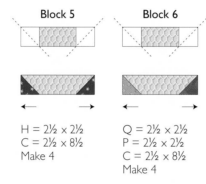

Block 5   Block 6

H = 2½ × 2½   Q = 2½ × 2½
C = 2½ × 8½   P = 2½ × 2½
Make 4   C = 2½ × 8½
                Make 4

11. Sew Block 5 unit from step 9 between two Block 5 units from step 10 as shown. Press. Repeat using Block 6 units from steps 9 and 10.

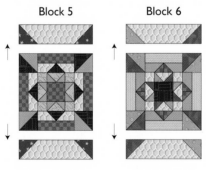

Block 5   Block 6

12. Sew one Block 5 unit from step 10 between two 2½" Fabric C squares as shown. Press. Make two. Sew Block 6 unit from step 10 between two 2½" Fabric C squares. Press. Make two.

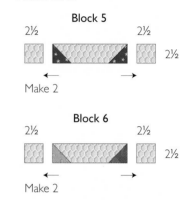

Block 5

2½   2½
                              2½

Make 2

Block 6

2½   2½
                              2½

Make 2

13. Sew Block 5 unit from step 11 between two Block 5 units from step 12 as shown. Press. Repeat using Block 6 units from steps 11 and 12. Blocks measure 12½" square.

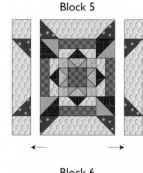

Block 5

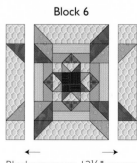

Block 6

Blocks measure 12½" square

PINWHEEL STAR

1. Draw diagonal line on wrong side of one 3" Fabric B square. Place marked Fabric B square and one 3" Fabric I square right sides together. Sew a scant ¼" away from drawn line on both sides to make half-square triangles. Make two. Cut on drawn line. Press. Square to 2½". This will make four half-square triangles. Label Block 7. Repeat using 3" Fabric L squares and 3" Fabric N squares. Make four half-square triangles. Label Block 8.

Block 7

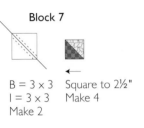

B = 3 × 3   ←
I = 3 × 3   Square to 2½"
Make 2   Make 4

Block 8

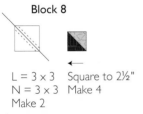

L = 3 × 3   ←
N = 3 × 3   Square to 2½"
Make 2   Make 4

2. Repeat step 1 using eight 3" Fabric B squares and eight 3" Fabric J squares. Make sixteen half-square triangles. You will use eight units each for Block 7 and Block 8.

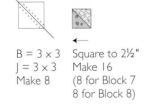

B = 3 × 3   ←
J = 3 × 3   Square to 2½"
Make 8   Make 16
(8 for Block 7
8 for Block 8)

3. Arrange and sew each Block 7 unit from step 1 as shown. Press. Arrange and sew each Block 8 unit from step 1 as shown. Press.

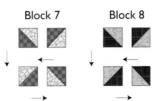

Block 7   Block 8

4. Arrange and sew one 2½" Fabric B square, two units from step 2, and one 2½" Fabric P square as shown. Press. Make four and label Block 7. Arrange and sew one 2½" Fabric B square, two units from step 2, and one 2½" Fabric I square as shown. Press. Make four and label Block 8.

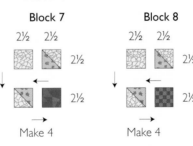

Block 7   Block 8
2½ 2½   2½ 2½
2½   2½
2½   2½
Make 4   Make 4

5. Refer to Quick Corner Triangles on page 108. Sew two 2½" Fabric B squares and two 2½" Fabric K squares to one 4½" Fabric Q square as shown. Press. Make four and label Block 7. Sew two 2½" Fabric B squares, one 2½" Fabric L square, and one 2½" Fabric N square to one 4½" Fabric O square. Press. Make four and label Block 8.

Block 7

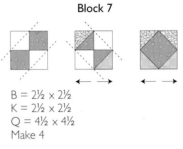

B = 2½ × 2½
K = 2½ × 2½
Q = 4½ × 4½
Make 4

Block 8

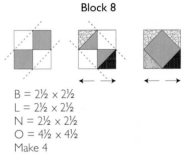

B = 2½ × 2½
L = 2½ × 2½
N = 2½ × 2½
O = 4½ × 4½
Make 4

6. Sew one Block 7 unit from step 5 between two Block 7 units from step 4 as shown. Press. Make two. Repeat using Block 8 units from steps 4 and 5.

Block 7

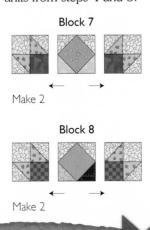

Make 2

Block 8

Make 2

57

7. Sew Block 7 unit from step 3 between two Block 7 units from step 5 as shown. Press. Repeat using Block 8 units from steps 3 and 5.

Block 7

Block 8

8. Sew Block 7 unit from step 7 between two Block 7 units from step 6 as shown. Press. Repeat using Block 8 units from steps 6 and 7. Blocks measure 12½" square.

Block 7

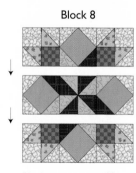

Block 8

Blocks measure 12½" square

CENTER BLOCK

1. Sew one 2½" Fabric J square between two 1½" x 2½" Fabric A pieces as shown. Press. Make four. Sew two 1½" x 4½" Fabric A pieces to sides. Press. Make four.

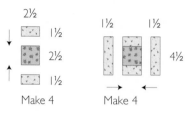

2½

↓ 1½
2½
↑ 1½

Make 4

1½   1½

4½

→   ←

Make 4

2. Sew one 2½" Fabric G square and one 2½" Fabric N square together as shown. Press. Make four. Sew one 2½" x 4½" Fabric G piece to side of unit as shown. Press. Make four.

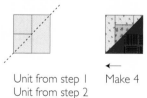

2½   2½

↑ 2½
2½   4½

←

Make 4   Make 4

3. Refer to Quick Corner Triangles on page 108. Sew one unit from step 2 to one unit from step 1 as shown. Prior to stitching, flip back unit to see if positioning is correct. Press. Make four.

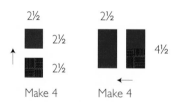

Unit from step 1   ←
Unit from step 2   Make 4

4. Making quick corner triangle units, sew two 2½" Fabric A squares and two 2½" Fabric K squares to one 4½" Fabric I square as shown. Press. Make four.

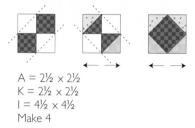

←   →

A = 2½ x 2½
K = 2½ x 2½
I = 4½ x 4½
Make 4

5. Making quick corner triangle units, sew four 2½" Fabric G squares to one 4½" Fabric D square as shown. Press.

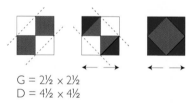

←   →

G = 2½ x 2½
D = 4½ x 4½

6. Sew one unit from step 4 between two units from step 3 as shown. Press. Make two.

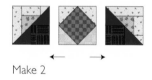

←   →

Make 2

7. Sew unit from step 5 between two units from step 4 as shown. Press.

→   ←

8. Sew unit from step 7 between two units from step 6 as shown. Press. Block measures 12½" square.

Block 9

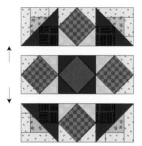

Block measures 12½" square

SASHING SQUARES

1. Sew one 4⅜" Fabric F square between two 1½" x 4⅜" Fabric E pieces as shown. Press. Sew two 1½" x 6⅜" Fabric E pieces to sides. Press. Make ten and label Unit 1. Sew one 4⅜" Fabric D square between two 1½" x 4⅜" Fabric E pieces as shown. Press. Sew two 1½" x 6⅜" Fabric E pieces to sides. Press. Make eight and label Unit 2.

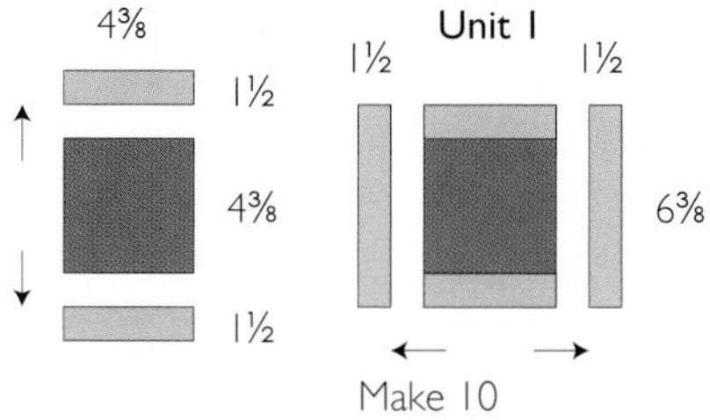

4⅜
1½
4⅜
1½

Unit 1
1½   1½
6⅜

Make 10

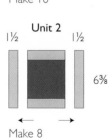

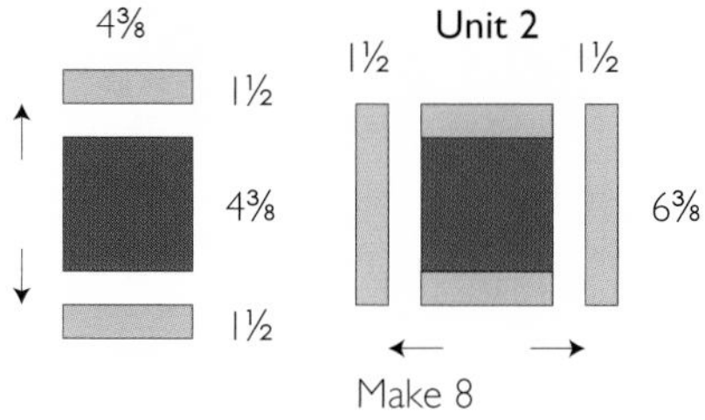

4⅜
1½
4⅜
1½

Unit 2
1½   1½
6⅜

Make 8

2. Sew one Unit 1 from step 1 between two 2" x 6⅜" Fabric D pieces as shown. Press. Sew two 2" x 9⅜" Fabric D pieces to sides. Press. Make ten. Sew one Unit 2 from step 1 between two 2" x 6⅜" Fabric F pieces as shown. Press. Sew two 2" x 9⅜" Fabric F pieces to sides. Press. Make eight.

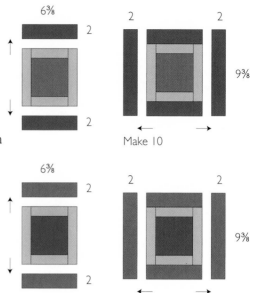

6⅜
2
2
2   2
9⅜
2

Make 10

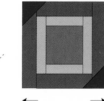

6⅜
2
2   2
9⅜
2

Make 8

3. Refer to Quick Corner Triangles on page 108. Sew two 3" Fabric G squares to Unit 1 from step 2 as shown. Press. Make ten. Cut on diagonal as shown to make twenty Unit 1 triangles. Sew two 3" Fabric H squares to Unit 2 from step 2 as shown. Press. Make eight. Cut diagonally as shown to make sixteen Unit 2 triangles.

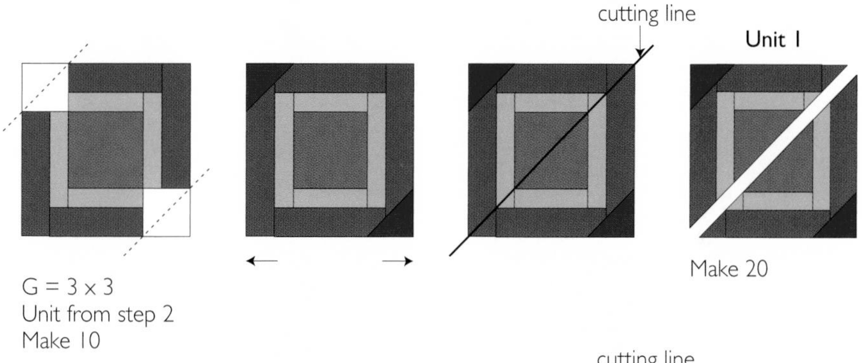

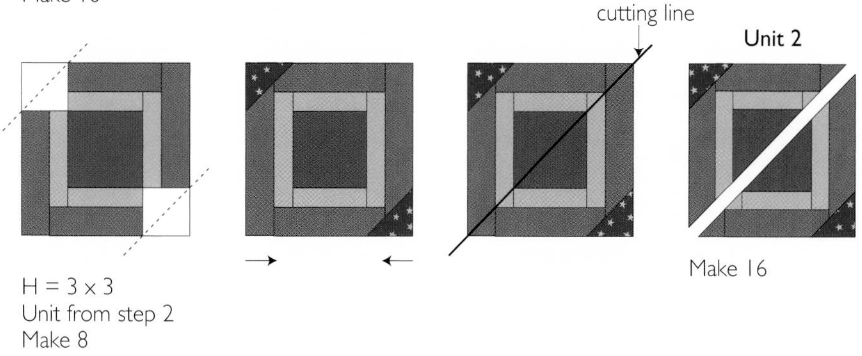

cutting line

Unit 1

Make 20

G = 3 x 3
Unit from step 2
Make 10

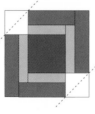

cutting line

Unit 2

Make 16

H = 3 x 3
Unit from step 2
Make 8

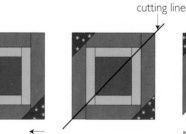

4. Referring to photo on page 50 and layout, sew four Unit 1 triangles to corner star blocks and Center Block as shown. Press. Sew four Unit 2 triangles to each remaining block. Press. *Note:* Triangles will extend past raw edge of square.

Block measures 17½" square

5. Refer to photo on page 50. Arrange and sew blocks in three horizontal rows of three blocks each. Press seams in opposite direction from row to row. Sew rows together. Press.

BORDERS

1. Refer to Quick Corner Triangles on page 108. Sew two 3" Fabric H squares to one 3" x 17½" First Border strip as shown. Press. Make eight. Sew two 3" Fabric G squares to one 3" x 17½" First Border strip. Press. Make four.

H = 3 × 3
First Border = 3 × 17½
Make 8

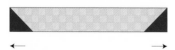

G = 3 × 3
Make 4

2. Making a quick corner triangle unit, sew one 3" Fabric G square to one 3" First Border square as shown. Press. Make four.

First Border = 3 × 3
G = 3 × 3
Make 4

3. Refer to photo on page 50. Sew one First Border/Fabric G unit from step 1 between two First Border/Fabric H units from step 1. Press. Make four.

4. Referring to photo, sew two border units from step 3 to top and bottom of quilt. Press seams toward border units. Sew units from step 2 to ends of remaining border units from step 3 checking position prior to stitching. Press seams toward border units. Sew to sides. Press.

5. Sew 1½" x 42" Second Border strips end-to-end to make one continuous 1½"-wide strip. Refer to Adding the Borders on page 110. Measure the quilt through center from side to side. Cut two 1½"-wide strips to that measurement. Sew to top and bottom of quilt. Press seams toward border.

6. Measure quilt through center from top to bottom, including borders just added. Cut two 1½"-wide Second Border strips to that measurement. Sew to sides of quilt. Press.

7. Refer to steps 5 and 6 to join, measure, trim, and sew 2½"-wide Third Border strips, 1½"-wide Fourth Border strips, and 2"-wide Fifth Border strips to top, bottom, and sides of quilt. Press seams toward newly added border strips.

8. Draw diagonal line on wrong side of one 5" Fabric H square. Place marked square and one 5" Sixth Border square right sides together. Sew a scant ¼" away from drawn line on both sides to make half-square triangles. Make two. Cut on drawn line. Press. Square to 4½". This will make four half-square triangles.

H = 5 × 5
Sixth Border = 5 × 5
Make 2

Make 4
Square to 4½"

9. Repeat step 8 using two 5" Fabric H and 5" Outside Border squares to make four half-square triangles. Repeat using four 5" Fabric G and 5" Outside Border squares to make eight half-square triangles. Press and square to 4½".

H/Outside Border
Make 4
Square to 4½"

G/Outside Border
Make 8
Square to 4½"

10. Arrange and sew one unit from step 8, one Fabric H/Outside Border unit and two Fabric G/Outside Border units from step 9 as shown. Press. Make four. Block measures 8½" square.

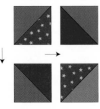

Make 4
Block measures 8½" square

11. Sew short ends of 4½" x 42" Sixth Border strips together in pairs. Make four. Repeat with 5" x 42" Outside Border strips. Sew Sixth Border strip and Outside Border strip together on long edges staggering seams to make border unit. Make four.

12. Refer to Adding the Borders on page 110. Measure quilt through center from side to side and from top to bottom, including borders already added. (These measurements should be the same.) Cut four border units to that measurement. Sew border units to top and bottom of quilt. Press seams toward border.

13. Referring to layout, sew blocks from step 10 to ends of remaining border units. Press. Sew to sides. Press.

LAYERING & FINISHING

1. Cut backing crosswise into three equal pieces. Sew pieces together to make one 92" x 120" (approximate) backing piece. Press and trim to 92" x 92".

2. Arrange and baste backing, batting, and top together, referring to Layering the Quilt on page 110.

3. Hand or machine quilt as desired.

4. Sew 2¾" x 42" binding strips end-to-end to make one continuous 2¾"-wide strip. Refer to Binding the Quilt on page 111 and bind quilt to finish.

AROUND THE BLOCK QUILT
Finished size: *84" x 84"*
Photo: *page 50*

PLAYFUL PiCNiC

53½" x 53½" • Quilt

Imagine a picnic where even the ants are welcome and you'll understand the charm of this colorful and clever throw. These industrious fellows are the result of super-simple digitized machine embroidery. Add a few quick-pieced slices of juicy watermelon–and you've got the makings of a summer's feast.

FABRIC REQUIREMENTS & CUTTING INSTRUCTIONS

Read all instructions before beginning and use ¼"-wide seam allowances throughout. Read Cutting Strips and Pieces on page 108 prior to cutting fabrics.

Playful Picnic Quilt 53½" x 53½"	FIRST CUT Number of Strips or Pieces	FIRST CUT Dimensions	SECOND CUT Number of Pieces	SECOND CUT Dimensions
Fabric A Sun Background ¼ yard	2	3½" x 42"	4 2 2 2	3½" x 6½" 3½" x 5½" 3½" squares 3½" x 2½"
Fabric B Side & Corner Setting Triangles ¾ yard	1 1	11¼" x 42" 10⅞" x 42"	2 2	11¼" squares* *cut twice diagonally to make Side Triangles. 10⅞" squares** **cut once diagonally to make Corner Triangles.
Fabric C Sun Center ¼ yard	1	8½" square		
Fabric D Light Sun Rays ⅛ yard	1	2½" x 42"	8	2½" squares
Fabric E Dark Sun Rays ⅛ yard	1	3½" x 42"	4	3½" squares
Fabric F Watermelon Rind & Sun Border ⅜ yard	1 4	4¾" x 42" 1½" x 42"	4 4 4 4	4¾" squares 1½" x 14½" 1½" x 8½" 1½" x 7½"
Fabric G Light Checks ⅙ yard	3	1½" x 42" (for strip piecing)		
Fabric H Dark Checks & Ant Border ¼ yard	3 2	1½" x 42" (for strip piecing) 1" x 42"	8 8	1" x 4½" 1" x 3½"
Fabric I Checkerboard Sashing ¼ yard	2	3½" x 42"	4	3½" x 14½"
Fabric J Watermelon Background ⅝ yard	2 2	6⅝" x 42" 1⅞" x 42"	8 8	6⅝" squares** **cut once diagonally 1⅞" x 8½"
Fabric K Watermelon ¼ yard	1	7½" x 42"	4	7½" squares

Playful Picnic Quilt continued	FIRST CUT Number of Strips or Pieces	FIRST CUT Dimensions	SECOND CUT Number of Pieces	SECOND CUT Dimensions
Fabric L Ant Background ¼ yard	1	7½" x 42" Embroider prior to cutting squares		Cut four 3½" squares after embroidering
Fabric M Ant Border ¼ yard	3	2" x 42"	8 8	2" x 7½" 2" x 4½"
BORDERS				
First Border ¼ yard	5	1½" x 42"		
Outside Border 2 yards (for bias) OR 1 yard	2 2 OR 5	5⅞" x 55" (bias strips) 5⅞" x 44" (bias strips) OR 5⅞" x 42"		
Binding ⅝ yard	6	2¾" x 42"		

Backing - 3⅜ yards
Batting - 60" x 60"
Seventeen Seed Buttons
Embroidery Thread or Floss

GETTING STARTED

This quilt includes two different 14½" square (unfinished) pieced blocks: one Sun Block and four Watermelon Blocks. The blocks are set on point, and the outside edges are finished with side and corner setting triangles. The side triangles—referred to in the instructions as Ant Triangle Blocks—combine piecing and digitized embroidery motifs. We cut the Fabric L background squares slightly oversized, and then trimmed them to 3½" after completing the embroidery. Refer to Preparing and Embroidering the Ant Blocks on page 65 for additional information. For an additional design element, we cut the Outside Border strips on the bias to take advantage of the fabric's printed motif. If you prefer to cut Outside Borders in the traditional fashion (across the fabric width), the yardage and cutting charts, as well as border instructions, cover this option as well.

Refer to Accurate Seam Allowance on page 108. Whenever possible, use the Assembly Line Method on page 108. Press seams in direction of arrows.

SUN BLOCK

1. Refer to Quick Corner Triangles on page 108. Sew four 2½" Fabric D squares to 8½" Fabric C square as shown. Press.

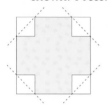

D = 2½ x 2½
C = 8½ x 8½

2. Making quick corner triangle units, sew one 3½" Fabric E square and one 2½" Fabric D square to one 3½" x 6½" Fabric A piece as shown. Press. Make four.

E = 3½ x 3½
D = 2½ x 2½
A = 3½ x 6½
Make 4

3. Sew one 3½" x 2½" Fabric A piece to one unit from step 2 as shown. Press. Make two.

2½

3½

Make 2

4. Sew unit from step 1 between two units from step 3 as shown. Press.

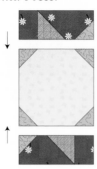

5. Sew one unit from step 2 between one 3½" x 5½" Fabric A piece and one 3½" Fabric A square as shown. Press. Make two.

5½   3½
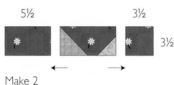
3½

Make 2

6. Sew unit from step 4 between two units from step 5 as shown. Press. Block measures 14½" square.

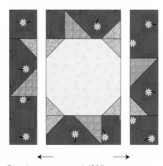

Block measures 14½" square

WATERMELON BLOCK

1. Sew two 1½" x 42" Fabric G strips and two 1½" x 42" Fabric H strips together as shown to make a strip set. Press. Cut twenty-four 1½"-wide segments.

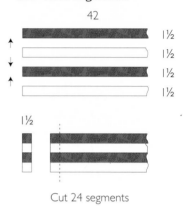

42

1½
1½
1½
1½

1½

Cut 24 segments

2. Sew one 1½" x 42" Fabric G strip and one 1½" x 42" Fabric H strip together as shown to make a strip set. Press. Cut eight 1½"-wide segments.

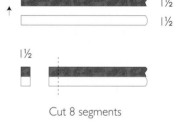

1½
1½

1½

Cut 8 segments

3. Sew three segments from step 1 and one segment from step 2 together as shown. Press. Make eight.

Make 8

4. Arrange and sew two units from step 3, one 3½" x 14½" Fabric I strip, and one 1½" x 14½" Fabric F strip together as shown. Press. Make four.

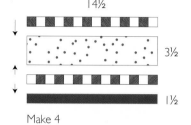

14½

3½

1½

Make 4

5. Making a quick corner triangle unit, sew one 4¾" Fabric F square to one 7½" Fabric K square as shown. Press. Make four.

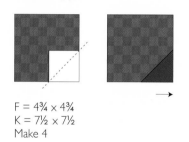

F = 4¾ x 4¾
K = 7½ x 7½
Make 4

6. Sew 1½" x 7½" Fabric F strip to bottom of each unit from step 5 as shown. Press. Sew 1½" x 8½" Fabric F strip to right side of each unit. Press. Make four.

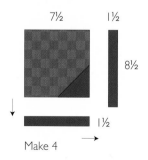

7½

1½

8½

1½

Make 4

7. Sew four Fabric J triangles to one unit from step 6 as shown. (Triangles will extend past raw edge of square.) Press. Make four. Square unit to 11¾".

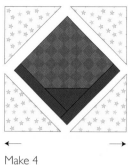

Make 4
Square to 11¾"

8. Measure 8½" from top edge of each unit from step 7 and trim as shown. Make four. Unit measures 11¾" x 8½".

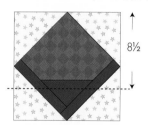

8½

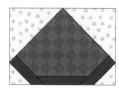

Make 4
Unit measures 11¾" x 8½"

9. Sew one unit from step 8 between two 1⅞" x 8½" Fabric J pieces as shown. Press. Make four.

1⅞   1⅞

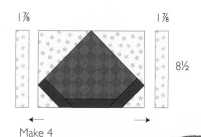

8½

Make 4

10. Sew units from steps 9 and 4 together in pairs as shown. Press. Make four.

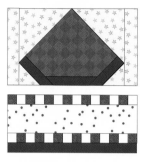

Make 4
Unit measures 14½" square

PREPARING & EMBROIDERING THE ANT BLOCKS

The ant motifs are embroidered on point on 7½" x 42" Fabric L strip. We scanned and digitized the embroidery pattern on page 66 using Bernina® Embroidery Software and a Bernina artista 200E. The ant fill was done with the step stitch, and legs and antennae with a satin stitch. A triple-stitch outline stitch was used to finish the embroidery.

If you prefer hand embroidery, refer to Embroidery Stitch Guide on page 111. Use three strands of embroidery floss and satin stitch for body and stem stitch for legs and antennae. After pieces are embroidered, and keeping ant on point, cut four 3½" squares as shown.

3½

3½

Cut 4

ANT TRIANGLE BLOCKS

1. Sew one embroidered ant square between two 1" x 3½" Fabric H pieces as shown. Press. Make four. Sew this unit between two 1" x 4½" Fabric H pieces as shown. Press. Make four.

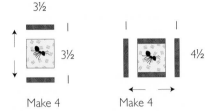

3½

3½

Make 4

4½

Make 4

2. Sew unit from step 1 between two 2" x 4½" Fabric M pieces as shown. Press. Make four. Sew this unit between two 2" x 7½" Fabric M pieces as shown. Press. Make four.

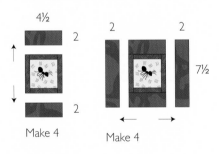

4½

2

2

2

2

2

7½

Make 4

Make 4

3. Sew two Fabric B Side Triangles to adjacent sides of one unit from step 2 as shown. Press. Make four.

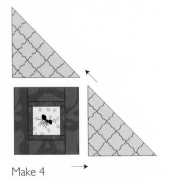

Make 4

ASSEMBLY

1. Arrange and sew two Fabric B Corner Triangles, two Watermelon Blocks, and Sun Block as shown. (Triangles will extend beyond raw edges of squares.) Press.

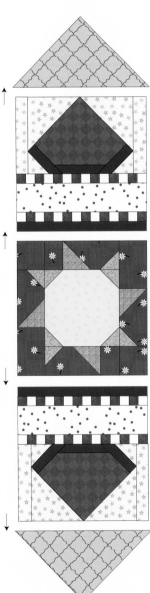

2. Sew one Watermelon Block between two Ant Triangle Blocks as shown. Press. Make two. Sew one Fabric B Corner Triangle to watermelon unit as shown. Press. Make two.

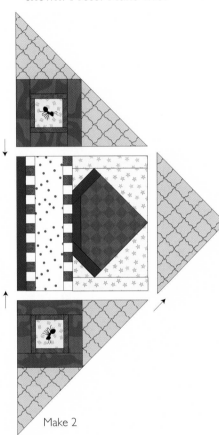

Make 2

3. Refer to photo on page 62 and layout. Sew unit from step 1 between two units from step 2. Press.

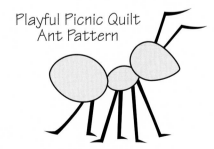

Playful Picnic Quilt
Ant Pattern

BORDERS

1. Sew 1½" x 42" First Border strips end-to-end to make one continuous 1½"-wide strip. Press. Refer to Adding the Borders on page 110. Measure quilt through center from side to side. Cut two 1½"-wide First Border strips to that measurement. Sew to top and bottom of quilt. Press seams toward border.

2. Measure quilt through center from top to bottom, including borders just added. Cut two 1½"-wide First Border strips to that measurement. Sew to sides of quilt. Press.

3. To add bias-cut Outside Border strips, refer to steps 1 and 2 to measure, trim, and sew 5⅞"-wide Outside Border strips to top, bottom, and sides of quilt. To minimize stretching, place Outside Border next to feed dog when stitching. Press seams toward Outside Border.

Tip: To eliminate excess seams, cut long bias strips from 2 yard piece of Outside Border fabric. Refer to Fussy Cut on page 108, prior to cutting a checked fabric.

Optional: For Outside Border strips cut on the straight grain, refer to steps 1 and 2 to join, measure, trim, and sew 5⅞"-wide Outside Border strips to top, bottom, and sides of quilt. Press seams toward Outside Border.

LAYERING & FINISHING

1. Cut backing crosswise into two equal pieces. Sew pieces together to make one 60" x 80" (approximate) backing piece. Press and trim to 60" x 60".

2. Arrange and baste backing, batting, and top together, referring to Layering the Quilt on page 110.

3. Hand or machine quilt as desired.

4. Referring to photo and layout, stitch seventeen seed buttons to watermelons as shown.

5. Sew 2¾" x 42" binding strips end-to-end to make one continuous 2¾"-wide strip. Refer to Binding the Quilt on page 111 and bind quilt to finish.

PLAYFUL PiCNiC QUiLT
Finished size: 53½" x 53½"
Photo: *page 62*

BUTTERFLIES & BEES

53" x 53" • Lap Quilt

The buzzin' of the bees and the gentle flutter of butterfly wings provide the perfect lullaby for a lazy afternoon spent napping under this delightful lap quilt. The blocks are fanciful, the button embellishment whimsical (as well as functional), and the construction is quick and simple!

FABRIC REQUIREMENTS & CUTTING INSTRUCTIONS

Read all instructions before beginning and use ¼"-wide seam allowances throughout. Read Cutting Strips and Pieces on page 108 prior to cutting fabrics.

Butterflies & Bees Lap Quilt 53" x 53"	FIRST CUT Number of Strips or Pieces	Dimensions	SECOND CUT Number of Pieces	Dimensions
Fabric A Block 1 Background ¾ yard	5	3½" x 42"	20 60	3½" squares 3½" x 2"
	1	2" x 42" (for strip piecing)		
	2	2" x 42"	40	2" squares
Fabric B Green Block Pieces ⅝ yard	4	3½" x 42"	25 20	3½" squares 3½" x 2"
	1	2" x 42" (for strip piecing)		
	1	2" x 42"	20	2" squares
Fabric C Button Background ¼ yard	2	3½" x 42" (for strip piecing)		
Fabric D Button Border & Butterfly Body Appliqués ⅙ yard	1	1½" x 42" (for strip piecing)		
	1	1½" x 42"	8	1½" x 4½"
Fabric E Button Border ⅛ yard	1	1½" x 42" (for strip piecing)		
	1	1½" x 42"	8	1½" x 4½"
Fabric F Bee & Butterfly Background ⅓ yard	1	5½" x 42"	2 4	5½" squares 4½" squares
	3	1½" x 42"	8 8	1½" x 6½" 1½" x 4½"
Fabric G Butterfly Wings ¼ yard	2	5½" "fussy cut" squares		
Fabric H Dark Checks ⅙ yard	3	1½" x 42" (for strip piecing)		
Fabric I Light Checks ⅙ yard	3	1½" x 42" (for strip piecing)		

Butterflies & Bees Lap Quilt continued	FIRST CUT Number of Strips or Pieces	Dimensions
BORDERS		
First Border ¼ yard	4	1½" x 42"
Second Border ¼ yard	4	1½" x 42"
Third Border ⅓ yard	5	1½" x 42"
Fourth Border ⅓ yard	5	1½" x 42"
Outside Border ¾ yard	5	4½" x 42"
Binding ⅝ yard	6	2¾" x 42"

Backing - 3⅜ yards
Batting - 59" x 59"
Bee Body, Head & Wing Appliqués - Assorted scraps
Lightweight Fusible Web - Scrap
Perle Cotton - Black & Gold
Twenty-one Assorted Buttons

GETTING STARTED

This quilt includes nine 12½" (unfinished) blocks: five of Block 1 and four of Block 2. Block 1 is a simple block constructed using Quick Corner Triangles. Block 2 combines a variety of techniques, including quarter-square triangles, a strip-pieced checkerboard border, and quick-fuse appliqué. Rather than traditional quilting, the layers of the quilt are secured with in-the-ditch stitching and buttons are tied through all layers with perle cotton. We left the thread tails long for a primitive look. Refer to Accurate Seam Allowance on page 108. Whenever possible, use the Assembly Line Method on page 108. Press seams in direction of arrows.

BLOCK 1

1. Referring to Quick Corner Triangles on page 108, sew two 2" Fabric A squares to one 3½" x 2" Fabric B piece as shown. Press. Make twenty.

A = 2 x 2
B = 3½ x 2
Make 20

2. Arrange and sew two units from step 1, two 3½" Fabric A squares, and one 3½" Fabric B square as shown. Press. Make five.

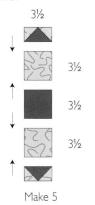

Make 5

3. Sew 2" x 42" Fabric A strip and 2" x 42" Fabric B strip together to make a strip set as shown. Press. Cut twenty 2"-wide segments.

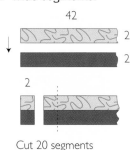

Cut 20 segments

4. Sew one 3½" x 2" Fabric A piece to one segment from step 3 as shown. Press. Make twenty.

Make 20

5. Making a quick corner triangle unit, sew unit from step 4 to one 3½" Fabric B square as shown. Prior to stitching, flip back unit to see if positioning is correct. Press. Make twenty.

Unit from step 4
B = 3½ x 3½
Make 20

6. Arrange and sew two 3½" x 2" Fabric A pieces, two units from step 5, and one 3½" Fabric A square together as shown. Press. Make ten.

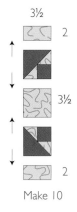

Make 10

7. Arrange and sew two 2" Fabric B squares, two 3½" x 2" Fabric A pieces, and one unit from step 1 together as shown. Press. Make ten.

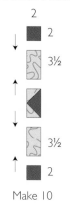

Make 10

8. Arrange and sew one unit from step 2, two units from step 6, and two units from step 7 as shown. Press. Make five. Block measures 12½" square.

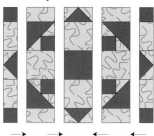

Make 5
Block measures 12½" square

BLOCK 2

1. Sew one 3½" x 42" Fabric C strip and one 1½" x 42" Fabric D strip together to make a strip set as shown. Press. Cut eight 3½"-wide segments.

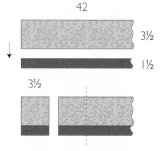

Cut 8 C/D segments

2. Sew one 3½" x 42" Fabric C strip and one 1½" Fabric E strip together to make a strip set as shown. Press. Cut eight 3½"-wide segments.

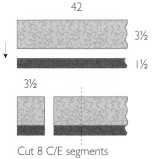

42

3½

1½

3½

Cut 8 C/E segments

3. Sew 1½" x 4½" Fabric D piece to each segment from step 1 as shown. Press. Make eight. Sew 1½" x 4½" Fabric E piece to each segment from step 2 as shown. Press. Make eight.

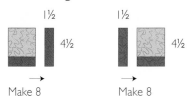

1½   1½

4½   4½

Make 8   Make 8

4. Draw diagonal line on wrong side of one 5½" Fabric F square. Place marked Fabric F square and one 5½" Fabric G square right sides together. Sew scant ¼" away from drawn line on both sides to make half-square triangles. Make two. Cut on drawn line. Press seams open. This will make four half-square-triangle units.

F = 5½ x 5½
G = 5½ x 5½
Make 2

5. Draw diagonal line on wrong side of unit from step 4 in opposite direction from seam as shown. Place right sides together with unmarked unit from step 4, matching seams and placing Fabric F triangle on top of Fabric G triangle. Sew scant ¼" from drawn line on both sides. Make two. Cut on drawn line. Press seams open. Square to 4½". This will make four quarter-square-triangle units, two of each variation.

Make 2

Make 4
(2 of each variation)
Square to 4½

6. Sew one unit from step 5 between two 1½" x 4½" Fabric F pieces as shown. Press. Sew two 1½" x 6½" Fabric F pieces to sides. Press. Make four, two of each variation.

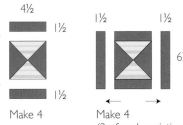

4½
1½
1½

1½   1½

6½

Make 4   Make 4
(2 of each variation)

7. Sew two 1½" x 42" Fabric H strips and two 1½" x 42" Fabric I strips together as shown to make a strip set. Press. Cut twenty-four 1½"-wide segments.

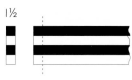

42
1½
1½
1½
1½

1½

Cut 24 segments

8. Sew one 1½" x 42" Fabric H strip and one 1½" x 42" Fabric I strip together as shown to make a strip set. Press. Cut eight 1½"-wide segments.

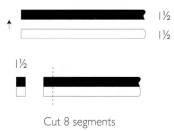

1½
1½

1½

Cut 8 segments

9. Sew one unit from step 7 and one unit from step 8 together as shown. Press. Make eight.

Make 8

10. Sew two units from step 7 together as shown. Press. Make eight.

Make 8

11. Sew unit from step 6 between two units from step 9 as shown. Press. Make four.

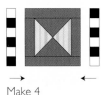

Make 4

12. Sew units from step 10 to top and bottom of unit from step 11 as shown. Re-press seams as necessary. Make four.

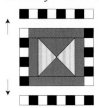

Make 4
Re-press as necessary

13. Sew one of each unit from step 3 together as shown. Press. Make eight.

Make 8

14. Sew one unit from step 12 to one unit from step 13 as shown. Press. Make four.

Make 4

15. Sew one unit from step 13 to one 4½" Fabric F square as shown. Press. Make four.

4½

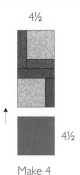

4½

Make 4

16. Sew unit from step 15 to unit from step 14 as shown. Press. Make four. Block measures 12½" square.

Make 4
Block measures 12½" square

ADDING THE APPLIQUÉS

Refer to appliqué instructions on page 109. Our instructions are for Quick-Fuse Appliqué, but if you prefer hand appliqué, reverse pattern and add ¼"-wide seam allowances.

1. Trace patterns below for *Bee* Appliqués (4 pieces) and *Butterfly* Body. Use Fabric D to trace and cut four *Butterfly* Body appliqué pieces. Use assorted scraps to trace and cut four each of all *Bee* appliqué pieces.

2. Refer to photo on page 68 and layout to position and fuse appliqués. Finish appliqué edges with machine satin stitch or other decorative stitching as desired.

Butterflies & Bees Lap Quilt Patterns
Patterns are reversed for use with Quick-Fuse Appliqué (page 109).

Tracing Line ——————
Tracing Line – – – – – – –
(will be hidden behind other fabrics)
Embroidery Line ··········

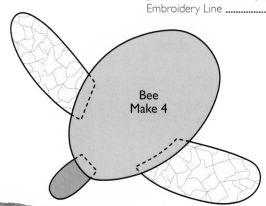

Bee
Make 4

Butterfly Body
Make 4

ASSEMBLY

Refer to photo on page 68 and layout. Arrange and sew blocks in three rows of three blocks each, alternating blocks as shown. Press seams in opposite directions from row to row. Sew rows together. Press.

BORDERS

1. Refer to Adding the Borders on page 110. Measure quilt through center from side to side. Cut two 1½" x 42" First Border strips to that measurement. Sew to top and bottom of quilt. Press seams toward border.

2. Measure quilt through center from top to bottom, including borders just added. Cut two 1½"-wide First Border strips to that measurement. Sew to sides of quilt. Press.

3. Refer to step 1 and 2 to measure, trim, and sew 1½"-wide Second Border strips to top, bottom, and sides of quilt. Press seams toward Second Border strips.

4. Sew 1½" x 42" Third Border strips end-to-end to make one continuous 1½"-wide strip. Press. Refer to steps 1 and 2 to measure, trim, and sew 1½"-wide Third Border strips to top, bottom, and sides of quilt. Press seams toward Third Border strips.

5. Repeat step 4 to join, measure, trim, and sew 1½"-wide Fourth Border strips and 4½"-wide Outside Border strips to top, bottom, and sides of quilt. Press seams toward each newly added border.

LAYERING & FINISHING

1. Cut backing crosswise into two equal pieces. Sew pieces together to make one 61" x 80" (approximate) backing piece. Press and trim to 61" x 61".

2. Arrange and baste backing, batting, and top together, referring to Layering the Quilt on page 110.

3. Hand or machine quilt as desired. We quilted in-the-ditch around each block, and added minimal in-the-ditch stitching as needed to secure the layers. Buttons tied through all layers will also secure the quilt.

4. Refer to photo on page 68 and layout and use gold perle cotton thread to tie quilt, adding buttons to each block as shown. Leave long tails (about ¾") for a primitive look.

5. Refer to Embroidery Stitch Guide on page 111. Use black perle cotton or two strands of embroidery floss and a running stitch to add butterfly antennae.

6. Sew 2¾" x 42" binding strips end-to-end to make one continuous 2¾"-wide strip. Refer to Binding the Quilt on page 111 and bind quilt to finish.

BUTTERFLIES & BEES LAP QUILT

Finished size: 53" x 53"
Photo: page 68

ARGYLE COMFORTER

67" x 79½" • Quilt

Lucky the little lad or lassie who snuggles beneath this bonny bed quilt. Good news for the quilter too: despite its complex good looks, you'll find this cozy comforter surprisingly simple to stitch. Easy strip-piecing duplicates the look of intricate argyle plaid.

FABRIC REQUIREMENTS & CUTTING INSTRUCTIONS

Read all instructions before beginning and use ¼"-wide seam allowances throughout. Read Cutting Strips and Pieces on page 108 prior to cutting fabrics.

Argyle Comforter Quilt 67" x 79½"	FIRST CUT		SECOND CUT	
	Number of Strips or Pieces	Dimensions	Number of Pieces	Dimensions
Fabric A *Light Background* 1¾ yards	13	4½" x 42"		
Fabric B *Dark Background* 1¾ yards	13	4½" x 42"		
Fabric C *Lattice* ⅞ yard	20	1¼" x 42"	2 2 2 2 2 38	1¼" x 74"** 1¼" x 56"** 1¼" x 38" 1¼" x 20" 1¼" x 10" 1¼" x 8½" **Pieced Strips*
BORDERS				
First Border ½ yard	6	2½" x 42"		
Second Border ⅜ yard	7	1½" x 42"		
Outside Border 2½ yards** (directional) OR 1¼ yards (non-directional)	2 2 7	84" x 5½" 78" x 5½" OR 5½" x 42"		
Binding ⅔ yard	8	2¾" x 42"		

Backing - 4⅞ yards
Batting - 75" x 87"
Scottie Dog Appliqués - ⅓ yard each of two fabrics
Lightweight Fusible Web - 1¼ yards

**For directional fabric, the measurement that is listed first runs parallel to selvage. Extra fabric provided for mitering.

GETTING STARTED

This quilt includes forty-nine 8½" (unfinished) Four Patch blocks, all constructed from a basic two-fabric strip set. The completed blocks are pieced with sashing into staggered horizontal rows, and then the entire quilt center is turned on point to create a diagonal—or plaid—effect. The edges of the quilt are trimmed after the First Border strips are added. Note that some of the sashing strips are cut longer than the rows to allow extra length for this trimming step.

We used a lengthwise stripe for the Outside Border and mitered the corners for a wonderful picture-frame finish. If you prefer to use non-directional fabric, the yardage, cutting chart, and border instructions, cover this option as well.

Refer to Accurate Seam Allowance on page 108. Whenever possible, use Assembly Line Method on page 108. Press seams in direction of arrows.

MAKING THE ROWS

1. Sew one 4½" x 42" Fabric A strip and one 4½" x 42" Fabric B strip together as shown to make a strip set. Press. Make thirteen strip sets. Cut ninety-eight 4½"-wide segments.

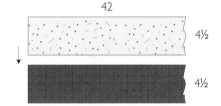

Make 13

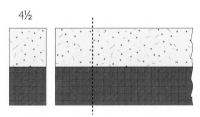

Cut 98 segments

2. Sew two segments from step 1 together as shown. Press. Make forty-nine blocks.

Make 49
Block measures 8½" square

3. Sew one 1¼" x 10" Fabric C piece between two 8½" square blocks from step 2 as shown. **Do not trim sashing.** Press. Make two and label Row 1.

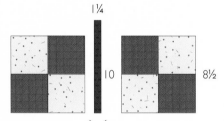

Make 2
(Label Row 1)

4. Sew one 1¼" x 8½" Fabric C piece between two blocks from step 2 as shown. Press. Make twenty-two.

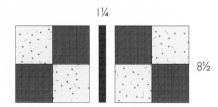

Make 22

5. Sew one 1¼" x 8½" Fabric C piece between two units from step 4 as shown. Press. Make ten. Label two of the units Row 2.

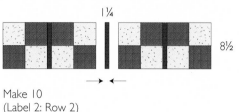

Make 10
(Label 2: Row 2)

6. Sew one 1¼" x 8½" Fabric C piece between one unit from step 5 and one unit from step 4 as shown. Press. Make two and label Row 3.

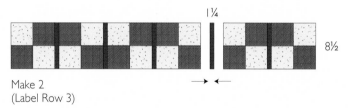

Make 2
(Label Row 3)

7. Sew one 1¼" x 8½" Fabric C piece between two units from step 5 as shown. Press. Make three. Label two of the units Row 4.

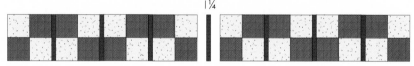

Make 3
(Label 2: Row 4)

8. Sew one 1¼" x 8½" Fabric C piece and one block from step 2 to right edge of remaining unit from step 7 as shown. Press and label Row 5.

(Label Row 5)

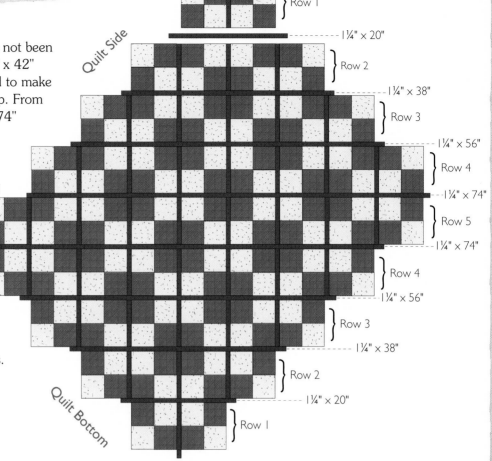

ASSEMBLY

1. If long Lattice strips have not been prepared, sew seven 1¼" x 42" Fabric C strips end-to-end to make one 1¼"-wide Lattice strip. From this strip, cut two 1¼" x 74" strips and two 1¼" x 56" strips. Refer to photo on page 74 and diagram at right. Arrange Rows 1–5; 1¼" x 20" Fabric C strips; 1¼" x 38" Fabric C strips; 1¼" x 56" Fabric C strips; and 1¼" x 74" Fabric C strips, staggering them as shown.

2. Sew rows together. Press.

In the diagram (top to bottom): Row 1; 1¼" x 20"; Row 2; 1¼" x 38"; Row 3; 1¼" x 56"; Row 4; 1¼" x 74"; Row 5; 1¼" x 74"; Row 4; 1¼" x 56"; Row 3; 1¼" x 38"; Row 2; 1¼" x 20"; Row 1. Labeled Quilt Side and Quilt Bottom.

BORDERS

1. Sew 2½" x 42" First Border strips end-to-end to make one continuous 2½"-wide strip. Press. From this strip, cut two 2½" x 50½" and two 2½" x 67" strips.

2. Use a see-through ruler and align the ¼" mark at center of blocks. Draw a line at edge of ruler ¼" beyond block centers on all four sides of quilt top. With right sides together and using alignment guidelines shown in red, sew 2½" x 50½" First Border strips to top and bottom of quilt. Trim excess quilt top even with long raw edge of border strip. Fold border away from quilt top and press seams toward border.

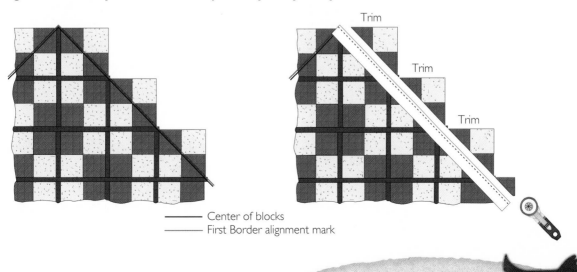

Trim   Trim   Trim

——— Center of blocks
——— First Border alignment mark

3. Refer to step 2 to sew 2½" x 67" First Border strips to sides of quilt. Trim blocks and press border.

4. Sew 1½" x 42" Second Border strips end-to-end to make one continuous 1½"-wide strip. Press. Refer to Adding Borders on page 110. Measure quilt through center from side to side, including borders just added. Cut two 1½"-wide Second Border strips to that measurement. Sew to top and bottom of quilt. Press seams toward newly added border.

5. Measure quilt through center from top to bottom, including borders just added. Cut two 1½"-wide Second Border strips to that measurement. Sew to sides of quilt. Press.

6. If using directional fabric, refer to Mitered Borders on page 110. Sew 78" x 5½" Outside Border strips to top and bottom and 84" x 5½" Outside Border strips to sides of quilt, mitering corners.

   If using non-directional fabric, refer to steps 4 and 5 to join, measure, trim and sew 5½"-wide Outside Border strips to top bottom and sides of quilt.

ADDING THE APPLIQUÉS

Refer to appliqué instructions on page 109. Our instructions are for Quick-Fuse Appliqué, but if you prefer hand appliqué, add ¼"-wide seam allowances.

1. Use patterns on pages 79-80 to make template for Scottie Dog. Trace and cut two Scottie Dog appliqués from each Scottie Dog Fabric.

2. Refer to photo on page 74 and layout to position and fuse appliqués. Finish appliqué edges with machine satin stitch or other decorative stitching as desired.

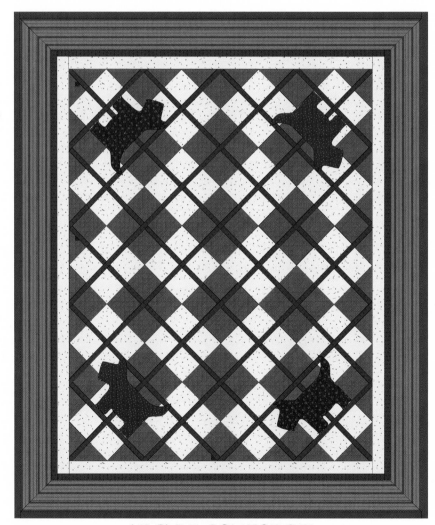

ARGYLE COMFORTER
Finished size: 67" x 79½"
Photo: page 74

LAYERING & FINISHING

1. Cut backing crosswise into two equal pieces. Sew pieces together to make one 87" x 80" (approximate) backing piece. Press.

2. Arrange and baste backing, batting, and top together, referring to Layering the Quilt on page 110.

3. Hand or machine quilt as desired.

4. Sew 2¾" x 42" binding strips end-to-end to make one continuous 2¾"-wide strip. Refer to Binding the Quilt on page 111 and bind quilt to finish.

Grain Line for Scottie Dog Pillow

Scottie Dog Appliqué Pattern
Patterns are reversed for use with Quick-Fuse Appliqué (page 109).

Tracing Line ——————
Placement Line _ _ _ _ _ _ _

Tracing Alterations _ _ _ _ _ _ _
(For Scottie Dog Pillow on page 81)

79

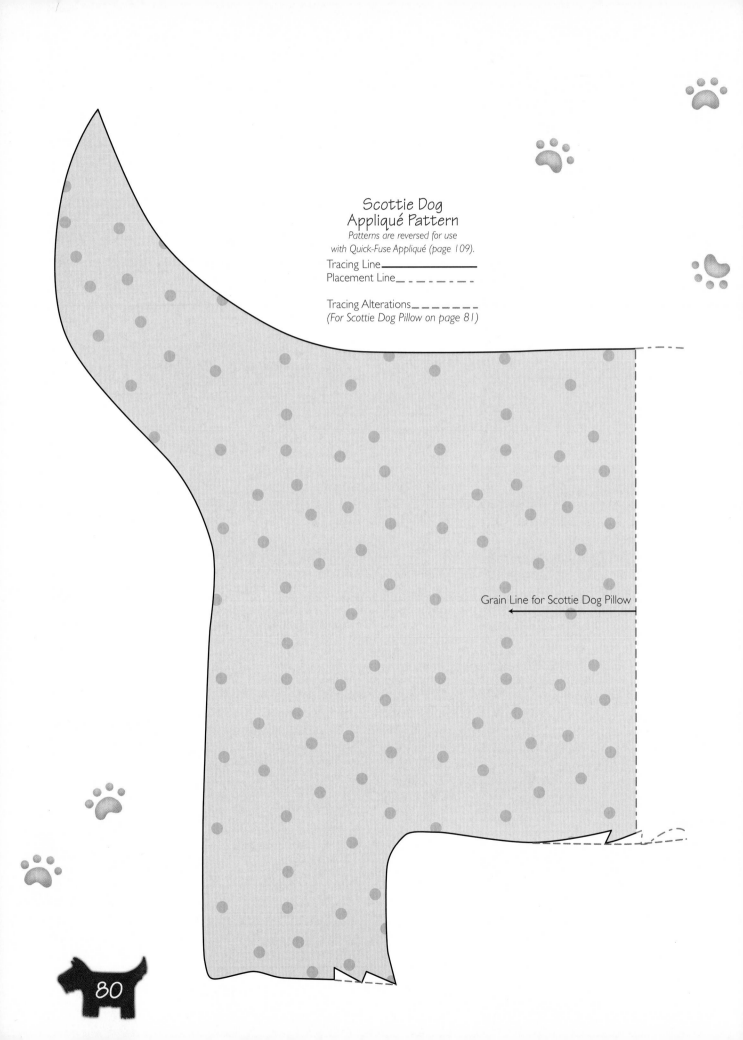

Scottie Dog
Appliqué Pattern
*Patterns are reversed for use
with Quick-Fuse Appliqué (page 109).*

Tracing Line⸺⸺⸺⸺
Placement Line⸻ ⸻ ⸻ ⸻

Tracing Alterations⸺ ⸺ ⸺ ⸺
(For Scottie Dog Pillow on page 81)

Grain Line for Scottie Dog Pillow ⟵

Scottie Dog Pillow

Snuggle with this furry friend that perfectly matches the Argyle Comforter. The same scottie dog pattern is used ... just enlarged and simplified. A cocky plaid bow provides the finishing touch to this cuddly companion.

MATERIALS NEEDED:

Fabric A (Scottie Body) - ⅝ yard

Fabric B (Bow Tie) - ⅛ yard
  3" x 31" piece

Polyester Fiberfill

Two ⅜ " Black Buttons or
  Black Perle Cotton

150% Enlargement of Scottie Pattern
(pages 79 & 80)

MAKING THE PILLOW

1. Join pieces of Scottie Pattern and smooth ruffled areas on muzzle, abdomen, and feet by following green lines as indicated.

2. Trace pattern from step 1 on wrong side of Fabric A placing Grain Line parallel to selvage (lengthwise grain) to minimize stretch. Place traced fabric, right sides together, with matching piece of Fabric A.

3. Sew ON traced line leaving a 4" opening for turning. Cut out Scottie ⅜" beyond traced line. Clip corners and curves and turn right side out.

4. Stuff Scottie lightly with polyester fiberfill. Refer to Embroidery Stitch Guide on page 111 and sew opening closed with a blind stitch.

5. Fold 3" x 31" Fabric B lengthwise, right sides together. Using a ¼"-wide seam, sew as shown leaving a 3" opening for turning.

Fold

6. Clip corners, turn right side out, and press. Referring to Embroidery Stitch Guide on page 111, blind stitch opening closed. Finished size is 1¼" x 30½".

7. Referring to photo, tie a bow around Scottie's neck.

8. Sew a button on each side of Scottie's face for eyes. If Scottie is for a small child, omit buttons and refer to Embroidery Stitch Guide on page 111 and use Perle cotton to make French knots for eyes.

Finished size: 18" x 13"

SPiNDRiFT

83" x 107" • Bed Quilt

Crisp geometry—reminiscent of nautical flags a-snap in the breeze—and an eye-catching color scheme combine to give this super-sharp quilt a masculine, seaworthy flair. You'll discover the "how"—a balanced blend of quick corner triangles and paper-piecing techniques—of smooth sailing as well.

FABRIC REQUIREMENTS & CUTTING INSTRUCTIONS

Read all instructions before beginning and use ¼"-wide seam allowances throughout. Read Cutting Strips and Pieces on page 108 prior to cutting fabrics.

Spindrift Bed Quilt 83" x 107"	FIRST CUT		SECOND CUT	
	Number of Strips or Pieces	Dimensions	Number of Pieces	Dimensions
Fabric A Background 3 yards	6 / 16 / 2	8½" x 42" / 3" x 42" / 2½" x 42"	24 / 96 / 10	8½" squares / 3" x 6" [P] / 2½" x 4½"
Fabric B Background 3 yards	3 / 28 / 2	4½" x 42" / 3" x 42" / 2½" x 42"	24 / 8 / 152 / 20	4½" squares / 3" x 9" [P] / 3" x 6" [P] / 2½" squares
Fabric C Star Background ⅞ yard	6	4½" x 42"	48	4½" squares
Fabric D Star Background, Star Center & Star Accent ⅞ yard	4 / 4	4½" x 42" / 2½" x 42"	26 / 6 / 48	4½" squares / 2½" x 4½" / 2½" squares
Fabric E Star ⅞ yard	7 / 2	3" x 42" / 2½" x 42"	40 / 20	3" x 6" [P] / 2½" squares
Fabric F Star & Diamonds 3 yards	13 / 11	5" x 42" / 3" x 42"	52 / 12 / 48	5" x 9" [P] / 3" x 9" [P] / 3" x 6" [P]
Fabric G Diamonds 1 yard	6	5" x 42"	24	5" x 9" [P]
Fabric H Star Center ⅓ yard	2	4½" x 42"	13	4½" squares
Fabric I Star Accent & Sixth Border Corners ⅓ yard	1 / 2	4½" x 42" / 2½" x 42"	4 / 24	4½" squares / 2½" squares

[P]-to be used for foundation paper-pieced diamonds

Spindrift Bed Quilt continued	FIRST CUT	
	Number of Strips or Pieces	Dimensions
BORDERS		
First Border & Binding 1¼ yards	10 / 7	2¾" x 42" (Binding) / 2" x 42"
Second Border ⅓ yard	7	1¼" x 42"
Third Border ⅝ yard	7	2¾" x 42"
Fourth Border ⅜ yard	8	1½" x 42"
Fifth Border ¾ yard	8	3" x 42"
Outside Border 1½ yards	9	5½" x 42"

Backing - 7⅝ yards
Batting - 91" x 115"

GETTING STARTED

Although it appears to be made from blocks, the center area of this quilt consists of quick corner triangle units and two different foundation paper-pieced diamond units, which are then assembled into rows. A series of simple borders frame the quilt. The Sixth Border is made from paper-pieced units, continuing the diamond motif. Refer to Accurate Seam Allowance on page 108. Whenever possible, use the Assembly Line Method on page 108. Press seams in direction of arrows.

ASSEMBLY

Two of the units for this quilt are paper-pieced Diamonds and Half-Diamonds. Copy patterns on page 88. If you are using a copier, be sure to compare the copy to the original pattern to make sure the copy is accurate. Make at least seventy-six copies of the Diamond Pattern and twenty copies of Half-Diamond pattern. Make all copies from the same copier at the same time to avoid distortions. Cut paper-piecing copies larger than the Trim Line on all sides. Units will be cut on Trim Line after they are completed.

1. Refer to Quick Corner Triangles on page 108. Sew one 4½" Fabric B square, one 4½" Fabric D square, and two 4½" Fabric C squares to one 8½" Fabric A square as shown. Press. Make twenty-four.

Fabric B = 4½ × 4½
Fabric D = 4½ × 4½
Fabric C = 4½ × 4½
Fabric A = 8½ × 8½
Make 24

2. Center paper-piecing Diamond Pattern printed side up, on wrong side of one 5" x 9" Fabric G piece as shown. Pin using large flower-head pin. Be sure Fabric G extends at least ½" on all sides of shape 1. If it is difficult to see through the paper, hold layers up to light to check fabric placement.

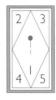

3. Fold paper along stitch line between sections 1 and 2. Trim fabric ¼" beyond Stitch Line as shown. Unfold paper.

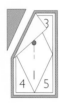

4. With right sides together, match edges of one 3" x 6" Fabric A piece with Fabric G piece just trimmed as shown. Hold layers up to light to see through to pattern line. Be sure both fabrics extend beyond trim line of pattern by at least ¼".

5. Turn paper printed-side up and sew through paper and both layers of fabric. Stitch on line as shown using a very short stitch (about 14 to 16 stitches per inch). Begin and end stitching ¼" beyond trim line.

6. Flip Fabric A piece over to cover seam line as shown. Press.

7. Repeat steps 3–6, trimming Fabric G between 1 and 3, and stitching another Fabric A piece. Press.

8. Repeat steps 3–6 to add 3" x 6" Fabric F pieces for shapes 4 and 5.

9. Turn unit from step 8 paper-side up, and stay-stitch just inside Trim Line, if desired, to secure fabric. Trim fabric along paper pattern Trim Line.

10. Repeat steps 2–9 to make twenty-four units using Fabrics G, A, and F and label Unit 1. Make fourteen units using Fabrics F, E, and A and label Unit 2; and thirty-eight units using Fabrics F and B and label Unit 3 as shown.

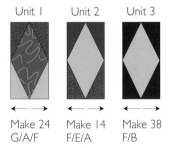

Unit 1	Unit 2	Unit 3
Make 24	Make 14	Make 38
G/A/F	F/E/A	F/B

11. Repeat steps 2–6 and step 9 using Half-Diamond pattern. Use one 3" x 9" Fabric B piece and one 3" x 6" Fabric A piece to make unit as shown. Make eight, four of each variation.

Make 8
(4 of each variation)

12. Repeat steps 2–7 and step 9 using Half-Diamond pattern, one 3" x 9" Fabric F piece, one 3" x 6" Fabric A piece, and one 3" x 6" Fabric E piece to make unit as shown. Make twelve units, six of each variation.

Make 12
(6 of each variation)

13. Making quick corner triangle units, sew four 2½" Fabric I squares to one 4½" Fabric H square as shown. Press. Make six and label Unit 4. Repeat using 2½" Fabric D squares and 4½" Fabric H squares to make seven and label Unit 5. Repeat using 2½" Fabric E squares and 4½" Fabric D squares to make two and label Unit 6. Repeat using 2½" Fabric B squares and 4½" Fabric I squares to make four and label Unit 7.

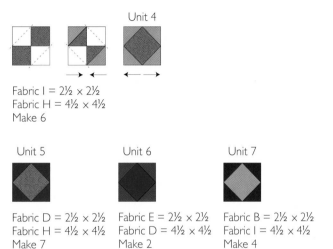

Unit 4

Fabric I = 2½ × 2½
Fabric H = 4½ × 4½
Make 6

Unit 5	Unit 6	Unit 7
Fabric D = 2½ × 2½	Fabric E = 2½ × 2½	Fabric B = 2½ × 2½
Fabric H = 4½ × 4½	Fabric D = 4½ × 4½	Fabric I = 4½ × 4½
Make 7	Make 2	Make 4

14. Making quick corner triangle units, sew two 2½" Fabric D squares to one 2½" x 4½" Fabric A piece as shown. Press. Make ten and label Unit 8. Repeat using 2½" Fabric E squares and 2½" x 4½" Fabric D pieces to make six and label Unit 9.

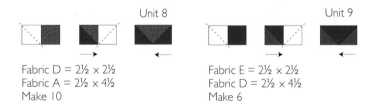

Unit 8

Unit 9

Fabric D = 2½ × 2½
Fabric A = 2½ × 4½
Make 10

Fabric E = 2½ × 2½
Fabric D = 2½ × 4½
Make 6

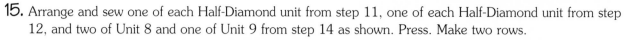

15. Arrange and sew one of each Half-Diamond unit from step 11, one of each Half-Diamond unit from step 12, and two of Unit 8 and one of Unit 9 from step 14 as shown. Press. Make two rows.

Make 2

16. Arrange and sew four units from step 1 and two of Unit 1 and one of Unit 2 from step 10 taking care to orient units as shown. Press. Make six rows.

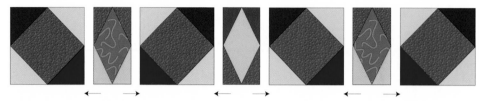

Make 6

17. Arrange and sew four of Unit 1 from step 10, and two of Unit 4 and one of Unit 5 from step 13 taking care to orient units as shown. Sew units together. Press. Make three rows.

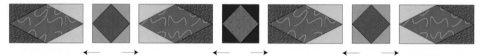

Make 3

18. Arrange and sew four of Unit 2 from step 10 and two of Unit 5 and one of Unit 6 from step 13 taking care to orient units as shown. Press. Make two rows.

Make 2

19. Referring to photo on page 82 and layout, arrange and sew together rows from steps 15-18. Press seams toward rows from step 16.

20. Arrange and sew together two 2½" Fabric B squares, one of each unit from step 11, two of each unit from step 12, three of unit 8 and two of unit 9 from step 14 as shown. Press. Make two.

2½   2½

2½

Make 2

21. Refer to photo on page 82 and layout. Sew units from step 20 to sides of unit from step 19, noting position of units. Press.

BORDERS

1. Sew 2" x 42" First Border strips end-to-end to make one continuous 2"-wide strip. Press. Refer to Adding the Borders on page 110. Measure quilt through center from side to side. Cut two 2"-wide First Border strips to that measurement. Sew to top and bottom of quilt. Press seams toward border.

2. Measure quilt through center from top to bottom, including borders just added. Cut two 2"-wide First Border strips to that measurement. Sew to sides of quilt. Press.

3. Refer to steps 1 and 2 to join, measure, trim, and sew 1¼"-wide Second Border strips, 2¾"-wide Third Border strips, 1½"-wide Fourth Border strips, and 3"-wide Fifth Border strips to top, bottom, and sides of quilt. Press seams toward each newly added border strip.

4. Referring to photo on page 82 and layout, sew together eight of Unit 3 from step 10, page 85, end-to-end. Press. Make two. Sew to top and bottom of quilt. Press seams toward Fifth Border strip. Sew together two of Unit 7 from step 13 and eleven of Unit 3. Press. Sew to sides of quilt. Press.

5. Refer to steps 1 and 2 to join, measure, trim, and sew 5½"-wide Outside Border strips to top, bottom, and sides of quilt. Press seams toward Outside Border.

LAYERING & FINISHING

1. Cut backing crosswise into three equal pieces. Sew pieces together to make one 91" x 120" (approximate) backing piece. Press.

2. Arrange and baste backing, batting, and top together, referring to Layering the Quilt on page 110.

3. Hand or machine quilt as desired.

4. Sew 2¾" x 42" binding strips end-to-end to make one continuous 2¾"-wide strip. Refer to Binding the Quilt on page 111 and bind quilt to finish.

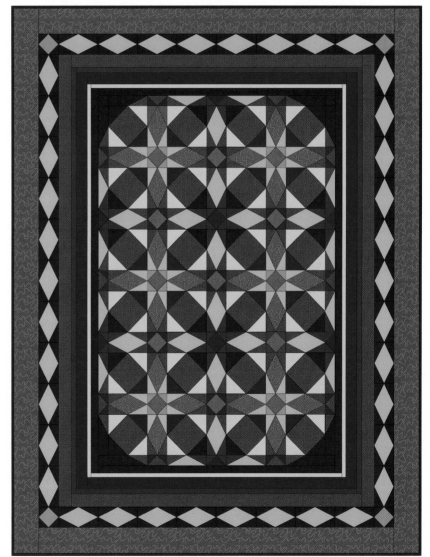

SPINDRIFT BED QUILT
Finished size: *83" x 107"*
Photo: *page 82*

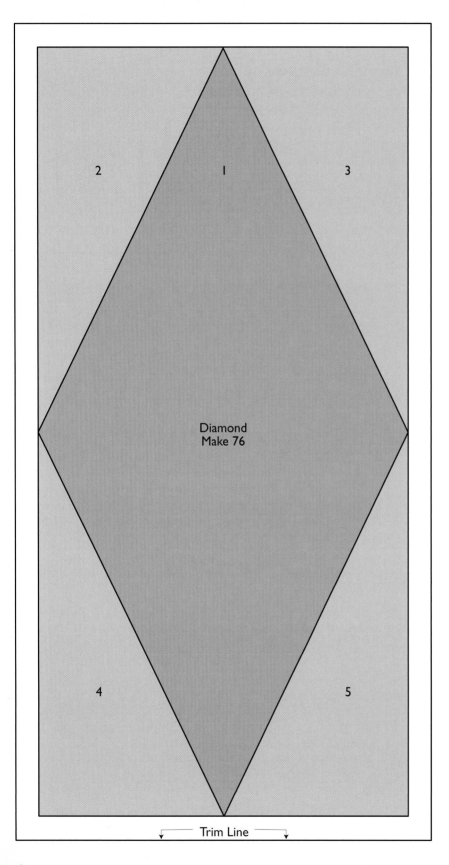

2   1   3

Diamond
Make 76

4   5

Trim Line

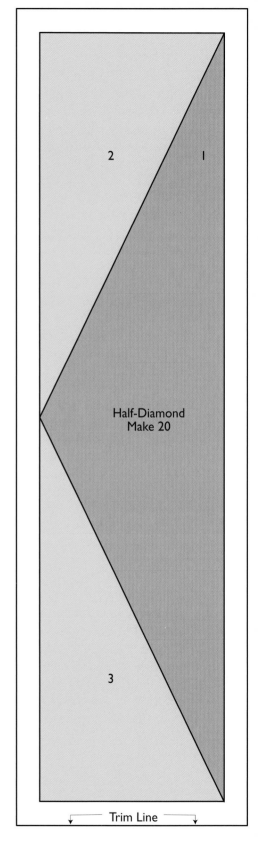

2   1

Half-Diamond
Make 20

3

Trim Line

Spindrift Bed Quilt
Paper-Piecing Patterns

*Permission to photocopy this page (88) is granted by Debbie Mumm, Inc. to aid in completion of the
Spindrift Bed Quilt. Compare photocopy to make sure size is an accurate 4½" x 8½" and 2½" x 8½"
before making multiple copies.*

Spindrift Pillow Sham

Spin the perfect combination for a dreamy drift of snuggly comfort when you pair pillow shams with the stylish Spindrift Bed Quilt. Diamond borders make the sham the perfect complement!

MATERIALS NEEDED FOR ONE SHAM

Fabric A (Background) - ½ yard
  One 22" x 16" piece
Fabric B (First & Outside Borders) - ⅞ yard
  Four 4½" squares
  Forty 3" x 6" pieces (for paper piecing)
  Eight 2½" squares
  Four 1½ x 4½" pieces
  Two 1¼" x 22" strips
  Two 1¼" x 17½" strips
Fabric C (Diamonds) - ½ yard
  Ten 5" x 9" pieces (for paper piecing)
  Two 4½" squares
Fabric D (Second Border) - ⅓ yard
  Two 2" x 23½" strips
  Two 2" x 20½" strips
Backing - 1⅛ yards
  Two 20" x 28½" pieces
Pillow - 26" x 20"

Finished size: 34" x 28"

MAKING THE PILLOW SHAM

1. Sew 22" x 16" Fabric A piece between two 1¼" x 22" Fabric B strips. Press seams toward Fabric B. Sew this unit between two 1¼" x 17½" Fabric B strips. Press.

2. Sew unit from step 1 between two 2" x 23½" Fabric D strips. Press seams toward Fabric D. Sew this unit between two 2" x 20½" Fabric D strips. Press.

3. Refer to Spindrift Bed Quilt Assembly steps 2-9 (page 84) and Diamond Paper-Piecing Pattern on page 88. Make ten copies of paper-piecing pattern and make unit using one 5" x 9" Fabric C piece on section one, and four 3" x 6" Fabric B pieces for sections 2-5. Make ten units.

4. Referring to layout, sew three units from step 3 alternating with two 1½" x 4½" Fabric B pieces as shown. Press. Make two borders and sew to top and bottom of sham. Press seams toward Second Border.

5. Referring to Spindrift Bed Quilt step 13 (page 85), make Quick Corner Triangle Units using one 4½" Fabric C square and four 2½" Fabric B squares. Press. Make two.

6. Referring to layout, arrange and sew two 4½" Fabric B squares, two units from step 3 and one unit from step 5. Press seams away from center. Make two. Sew units to sides of sham.

7. Refer to Finishing Pillows page 111, step 1 to quilt top. Refer to steps 2-4 to sew 20" x 28½" Backing pieces to pillow. Stitch in the ditch between Second and Outside Borders to create a flange. Insert pillow.

SUMMER SUN

57" x 57" • Beach Throw

With its sizzling suns and sporty flip-flop appliqués, this casual throw is the perfect companion piece for poolside or beach. We've made it with purchased towels, so it is as practical as it is playful. Make one for yourself…and one as a gift for your best beachcombing buddy!

Summer Sun Beach Throw 57" x 57"	FiRST CUT	
	Number of Strips or Pieces	Dimensions
This project can be made with four towels: Three bath towels measuring approximately 27" x 52" and one towel approximately 30" x 60". This will provide more fabric than is necessary, but most towels have decorative hems that will not be used.		
Fabric A* *Flipflop Center Background* **30" x 60" towel OR** 1⅔ yards *terrycloth*	1	15" x 57"
Fabric B* Center Block Accent **Towel Scraps OR** ⅓ yard *terrycloth*	2	4" x 15"
Fabric C* Corner Sun Backgrounds **Three 27" x 52" towels OR** ⅔ yard each of three terrycloth fabrics	4**	22" x 19½"
	**(Cut two pieces from one towel and one piece from each of two towels)	
Fabric D* Middle Sun Backgrounds **Towel or Fabric Scraps from Fabric C**	2	22" x 20"
	(Cut 1 piece from each of two towels)	
Fabric E Sashing & Outside Border/ Binding 2⅛ yards	6 / 5	7" x 42" (Border) / 6" x 42" (Sashing)
Accent Border ⅓ yard	5	2" x 42"
Sun Appliqués -¼ yard each of three fabrics Sun Ray Appliqués -⅛ yard each of three fabrics Flip Flop Appliqués -⅛ yard each of three fabrics Flip Flop Strap Appliqués - Scraps Lightweight Fusible Web - 2¼ yards Water Soluble or Tearaway Stabilizer (recommended) - 3 yards		

FABRIC REQUIREMENTS & CUTTING INSTRUCTIONS

Read all instructions before beginning. This project uses ½"-wide seam allowances. Read Cutting Strips and Pieces on page 108 prior to cutting fabrics.

GETTING STARTED

We made this throw from four purchased towels, but have included yardages for terrycloth fabric in the Cutting Chart if you prefer that option. There is no batting, backing, or quilting. Most pieces are sewn wrong sides together with ½"-wide seam allowances, and the exposed seams are covered on the front with folded sashing. The Outside Border and Binding are cut in single, wide strips from the same fabric. The strips are sewn to the front of the throw, turned to the back, and machine stitched from the back to finish. The towel fabric gives the throw body in the "faux" binding.

The appliqués are quick-fused. We recommend that you use a water soluble or tear away stabilizer on the back of the throw as the appliqués are stitched in place. See Adding the Appliqués on page 94 for additional information. Press seams in direction of arrows.

ASSEMBLY

1. With right sides together, position one 4" x 15" Fabric B strip 7½" from top edge of 15" x 57" Fabric A strip as shown. Sew ½" from top edge of Fabric B strip to attach to Fabric A. Flip Fabric B strip right side up toward top edge of Fabric A and baste using ⅜"-wide seam. Repeat to sew 4" x 15" Fabric B strip to opposite end of Fabric A strip.

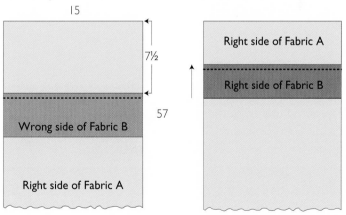

2. Sew 6" x 42" Fabric E strips end-to-end to make one continuous 6"-wide strip. Fold in half lengthwise with wrong sides together and press. Cut into two 57"-long strips and four 18"-long strips.

3. Refer to layout on page 94 and diagram. Layer 22" x 20" Fabric D piece (wrong side up), 22" x 19½" Fabric C piece (right side up), and center one 18"-long folded Fabric E strip, aligning long raw edges as shown. Sew layers together using ½"-wide seam. Make two, each in a different color combination.

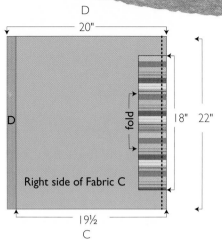

C = 22 x 19½
D = 22 x 20
Place toweling **wrong** sides together
Make 2 (1 of each combination)

4. Open units from step 3 so wrong sides of both Fabric C and Fabric D are face up. Repeat step 3 to sew one different-colored 22" x 19½" Fabric C piece and one 18"-long folded Fabric E strip to D side of one unit from step 3 as shown. Make two, one of each combination.

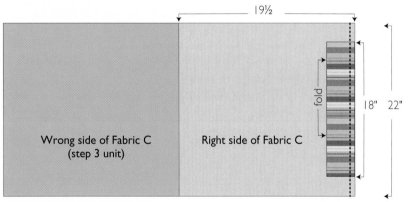

C = 22 x 19½
Unit from step 3

Make 2 (1 of each combination)

5. Open one unit from step 4 and turn it right side up as shown. Press Fabric E strips toward Fabric D piece to cover seams. Edge-stitch in place. Repeat for remaining unit from step 4.

6. Refer to layout on page 94 and diagram below. Layer one unit from step 5 (wrong side up), unit from step 1 (right side up), and one 57"-long Fabric E strip, aligning long raw edges as shown. Sew layers together using ½"-wide seam. Open unit so right sides of both Fabric C and Fabric D are face up. Repeat to sew remaining unit from step 5 to opposite side of unit from step 1.

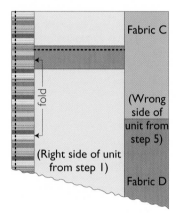

7. Open unit from step 6 and turn it right side up as shown. Press Fabric E strips toward Sun Background units, from step 5, to cover seams. Edge-stitch in place.

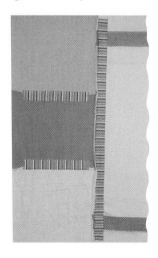

8. Sew 2" x 42" Accent Border strips end-to-end to make one continuous 2"-wide strip. Measure unit from step 7 from side to side and cut two 2"-wide Accent Border strips to that measurement. With right sides together, position one Accent Border strip 4½" from top edge of unit from step 7 as shown. Sew ½" from top edge of Accent Border strip to attach to unit. Repeat to sew trimmed 2"-wide Accent Border strip to bottom of unit. Flip Accent Border toward outside edge of unit to cover seam and press. Pin in place.

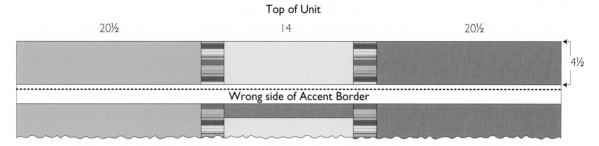

9. Measure unit from step 8 from top to bottom and cut two 2"-wide Accent Border strips to that measurement. With right sides together, position one Accent Border strip 4½" from side edge of unit as shown. Sew ½" from edge of Accent Border strip to attach to unit. Press Accent Border toward outside edge and pin in place. Repeat to sew, trim, press, and pin 2"-wide Accent Border strip to opposite side of unit.

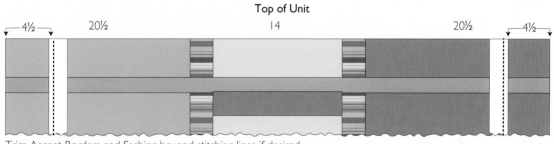

Trim Accent Borders and Sashing beyond stitching lines if desired.

10. Sew 7" x 42" Outside Border/Binding strips end-to-end to make one continuous 7"-wide strip. Measure unit from step 9 from side to side and cut two strips to that measurement. Turn under one long edge of each strip 1½" to wrong side and press. Place one strip right sides together with raw edge of top Accent Border (3½" from top edge of unit), aligning raw edges as shown. Sew ½" from edge of Outside Border/Binding strip to attach to unit. Repeat to sew 7"-wide Outside Border/Binding strip to bottom of unit. Flip border right side up and press toward outside edge of unit.

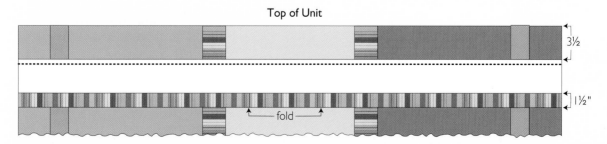

11. Measure unit from step 10 from top to bottom, including borders just added, and cut two 7"-wide Outside Border/Binding strips **3" longer** than that measurement to allow for 1½" folds. Turn under one long edge of each strip 1½" and press. Place one strip right sides together with raw edge of side Accent Border (3½" from side edge of unit), aligning raw edges. Sew ½" from edge of Outside Border/Binding strip to attach to unit. Repeat to sew 7"-wide Outside Border/Binding strip to opposite side of unit. Flip border right side up and press.

12. Turn folded edges of top and bottom Outside Border/Binding strips to back of unit then turn side Outside Border/Binding and pin in place. Stitch folded edge of Border/Binding from the back with ½"-wide seam to give appearance of ½"-wide binding.

Fold top and bottom binding in first, then sides

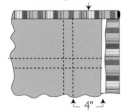

← 4" →

ADDING THE APPLIQUÉS

Refer to appliqué instructions on page 109. Our instructions are for Quick-Fuse Appliqué, but if you prefer hand appliqué, add ¼"-wide seam allowances.

1. Use patterns on page 95 to make templates for Sun Center, Sun Ray, and Flip Flop (2 pieces). Trace and cut six Sun Centers, forty-eight Sun Rays (eight for each Sun), and three and three reverse each of Flip Flop and Flip Flop Straps from appropriate fabrics. To reduce bulk, cut out center portion of fusible web for Sun Centers and Flip Flop appliqués by trimming inside traced lines as shown on patterns before adhering fusible to fabric.

2. Refer to photo on page 90 and layout to position appliqués on throw. Using water-soluble or tear away stabilizer on back side of throw, stitch appliqués with machine satin stitch or other decorative stitching as desired. Remove stabilizer.

SUMMER SUN BEACH THROW
Finished size: 57" x 57"
Photo: page 90

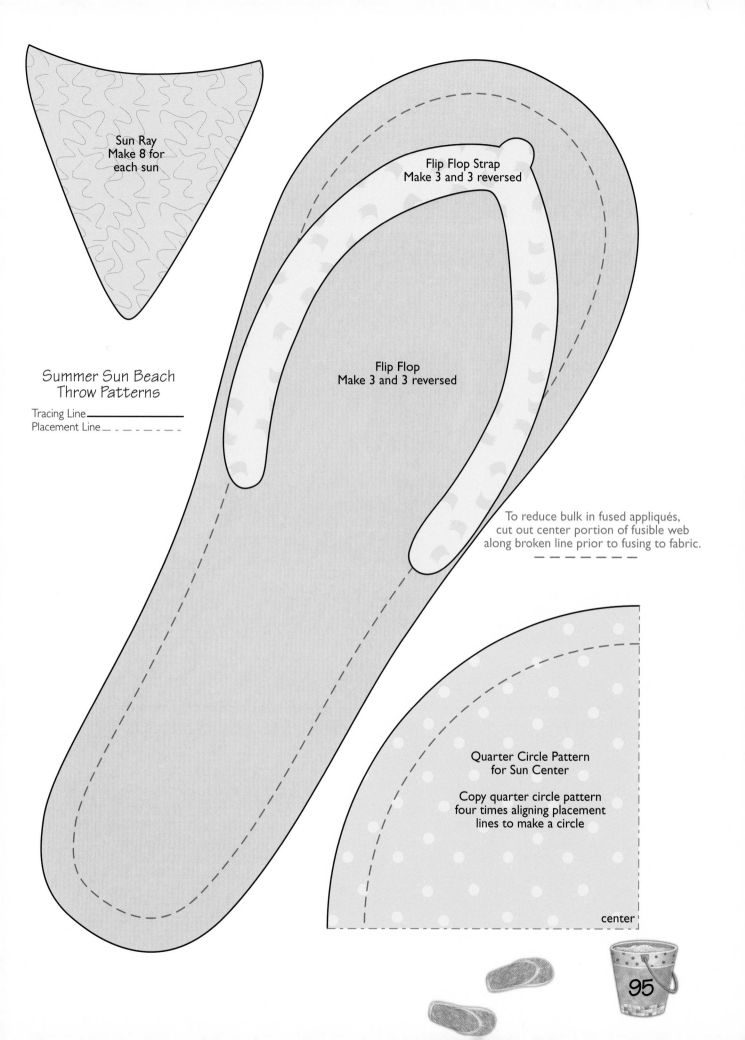

Sun Ray
Make 8 for
each sun

Flip Flop Strap
Make 3 and 3 reversed

Flip Flop
Make 3 and 3 reversed

Summer Sun Beach
Throw Patterns

Tracing Line ———————
Placement Line — — — — —

To reduce bulk in fused appliqués,
cut out center portion of fusible web
along broken line prior to fusing to fabric.
— — — — — — — — — —

Quarter Circle Pattern
for Sun Center

Copy quarter circle pattern
four times aligning placement
lines to make a circle

center

95

SUMMER TOTE

16" x 18" • Tote Bag

You'll be set for a day in the sun when you use this terry tote bag to carry your Summer Sun Beach Throw and other warm weather necessities. Computer clip art adds tropical appeal to the pocket.

MATERIALS NEEDED

*Fabric A (Tote Bag) -
One bath towel or ⅝ yard
terrycloth
  One 16½" x 37½" piece*

*Fabric B (Trim & Handle
Lining) - ½ yard
  Four 5½" squares
  Four 4½" squares
  Four 2" x 42" strips*

*Fabric C (Handle) - Towel
remnants or ⅓ yard
  Four 2" x 42" strips or
  enough 2"-wide strips sewn
  together end-to-end to make
  one 2" x 127½" strip*

*Washable Colorfast Printer
Fabric™ Sheet**

*Debbie Mumm® Summer Fun
Clip Art and Font CD
(Order at www.debbiemumm.com)*

**An 8½" x 11" piece of fabric may
be substituted*

MAKING THE TOTE

1. Refer to Fabric™ Sheet directions for printing clip art. Select design (we merged two images) and print on 8½" x 11" printer fabric. Set color as recommended. Turn top edge of printed fabric under ¼" and edge stitch along fold.

2. Refer to Sorbet Lap Quilt, page 38, steps 1 and 2 to sew two 5½" Fabric B squares to make four 4½" quarter-square triangles or if making Sorbet Lap Quilt, use four remaining 4½" units from step 2.

3. Arrange and sew two 4½" quarter-square triangles and two 4½" Fabric B squares as shown. Press. Fold under ¼" along one 16½" side and press. Make two.

4½   4½

      4½

Make 2

4. Arrange and pin right side of unit from step 3 to "wrong side" of 16½" x 37½" Fabric A piece. Stitch along 16½" edge. Press seam. Referring to photo, turn pieced unit to right side of Fabric A leaving ½" of Fabric A exposed as a trim.

5. Stitch close to folded edge of Fabric B unit to attach to Fabric A. Repeat steps 4 and 5 for opposite end of Fabric A.

6. Sew 2" x 42" Fabric B strips end-to-end to make one 2"-wide strip. Cut strip to 127½" long. Sew 2"-wide Fabric C strips end-to-end to make one 2" x 127½" strip. Press all seams open.

7. Sew strips from step 6, right sides together, along one 127½"-long side. With right sides together, sew short ends of handle together to form a long loop. Press seam open.

8. Fold raw edge of Fabric B under ¼" and press. Fold unit wrong sides together, so that a portion of each fabric is exposed on both sides of handle as shown.

9. Place Fabric C under folded edge of Fabric B as shown. Stitch close to edge of Fabric B.

10. Fold top and bottom edges of clip art printed fabric to achieve desired pocket height. Trim if needed.

11. Referring to photo, arrange and pin pocket on tote bag 1" below Fabric B Trim and equidistant from both sides of tote. Stitch bottom of pocket in place with a blind hem stitch or straight stitch.

12. Arrange and pin handle on tote as shown, covering side edges of pocket at least ½". With a blind hem stitch or straight stitch, sew both sides of handle to tote.

13. Fold tote in half crosswise, right sides together. Sew side seams. Turn right side out.

GUARDIAN ANGEL

48" x 68" • Crib Quilt

What better way to wish your precious little one "sweet dreams" than with a special, soft-as-a-cloud quilt? A bevy of appliqué angels and delicately embroidered floral motifs grace this darling quilt, sized perfectly for crib or nursery wall.

FABRIC REQUIREMENTS & CUTTING INSTRUCTIONS

Read all instructions before beginning and use ¼"-wide seam allowances throughout. Read Cutting Strips and Pieces on page 108 prior to cutting fabrics.

Guardian Angel Crib Quilt 48" x 68"	FIRST CUT		SECOND CUT	
	Number of Strips or Pieces	Dimensions	Number of Pieces	Dimensions
Fabric A Angel Background ¾ yard	1 6	5½" x 42" 3" x 42"	7 38	5½" squares 3" x 5½"
Fabric B* Embroidery Background ½ yard	2	8" x 42"	8	8" x 10" (trimmed to 5½" squares)
	*OR select a floral fabric and cut eight 5½" squares			
Fabric C Star ½ yard	5	3" x 42"	60	3" squares
Fabric D Star ¼ yard	2	3" x 42"	16	3" squares
Fabric E Angel Accent Border 1⅜ yards	3 12	3½" x 42" 3" x 42"	24 38 76	3½" squares 3" x 5½" 3" squares
Fabric F Accent Squares ⅜ yard	4	3" x 42"	48	3" squares
Fabric G Accent Triangles ⅓ yard	3	3½" x 42"	24	3½" squares
BORDERS				
First Border ¼ yard	5	1½" x 42"		
Second Border ⅞ yard	6	4½" x 42"		
Outside Border & Binding ⅞ yard	6 6	2¾" x 42" 1½" x 42"		

Backing - 3 yards
Batting - 54" x 74"
Angel Appliqués - Assorted Scraps
Embroidery Thread or Floss
Lightweight Fusible Web - 1 yard

GETTING STARTED

This quilt combines piecing, quick-fuse appliqué, and machine embroidery. It is constructed in units and rows rather than in blocks. The embroidery is stitched before the units and rows are assembled. We cut the Fabric B background pieces slightly oversized, and then trimmed them to 5½" after completing the embroidery. Refer to Embroidering the Flower Blocks below for additional information. We added the quick-fuse appliqués after the center of the quilt top was completed, but before adding the borders.

Refer to Accurate Seam Allowance on page 108. Whenever possible, use the Assembly Line Method on page 108. Press seams in direction of arrows.

EMBROIDERING THE FLOWER BLOCKS

The flower motifs on this quilt are embroidered on the 8" x 10" Fabric B pieces. We used a Bernina® artista 200E sewing machine and the Bernina artista CD The Good Life by Debbie Mumm®, pattern #24 (three and three reversed) and pattern #25 (one and one reversed). After pieces are embroidered, trim to 5½" square.

If you prefer hand embroidery, refer to Embroidery Stitch Guide on page 111 and pattern on page 103, and use three strands of embroidery floss and stem and satin stitches. Or, use a floral fabric and cut eight 5½" squares.

ASSEMBLY

1. Draw diagonal line on wrong side of one 3½" Fabric E square. Place marked Fabric E square and one 3½" Fabric G square right sides together. Sew scant ¼" away from drawn line on both sides to make half-square triangles. Make twenty-four. Cut on drawn line. Press and square to 3". This will make forty-eight half-square triangles.

E = 3½ x 3½
G = 3½ x 3½
Make 24

Square to 3"
Make 48

2. Refer to Quick Corner Triangles on page 108. Sew two 3" Fabric E squares to one 3" x 5½" Fabric A piece as shown. Press. Make thirty-eight.

E = 3 x 3
A = 3 x 5½
Make 38

3. Making quick corner triangle units, sew two 3" Fabric C squares to one 3" x 5½" Fabric E piece as shown. Press. Make thirty.

C = 3 x 3
E = 3 x 5½
Make 30

4. Making quick corner triangle units, sew two 3" Fabric D squares to one 3" x 5½" Fabric E piece as shown. Press. Make eight.

D = 3 x 3
E = 3 x 5½
Make 8

5. Arrange and sew four 3" Fabric F squares, four units from step 1, two units from step 2, and one unit from step 3 taking care to orient units as shown. Press. Make two.

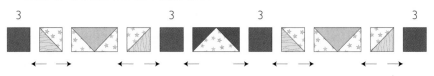

Make 2

6. Arrange and sew four 3" Fabric F squares, four units from step 1, two units from step 2, and one unit from step 4 taking care to orient units as shown. Press. Make four.

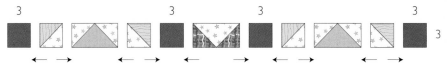

Make 4

7. Arrange and sew four units from step 1, four 3" Fabric F squares, two units from step 3, and one unit from step 2 taking care to orient units as shown. Press. Make six.

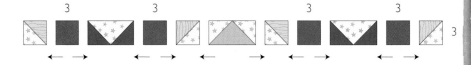

Make 6

8. Sew one unit from step 5 and one unit from step 7 together as shown. Press. Make two and label Rows 1 and 11.

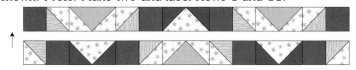

Make 2
Label: Rows 1 and 11

9. Sew one unit from step 7 and one unit from step 6 together as shown. Press. Make four and label Rows 3, 5, 7, and 9.

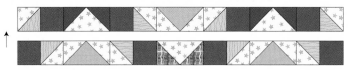

Make 4
Label: Rows 3, 5, 7, and 9

10. Arrange and sew four units from step 2, four units from step 3, two 5½" embroidered Fabric B squares, and one 5½" Fabric A square as shown. Press. Make three and label Rows 2, 6, and 10.

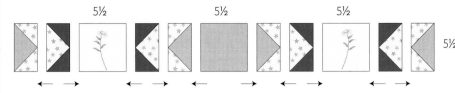

Make 3
Label: Rows 2, 6, and 10

11. Arrange and sew two units from step 3, four units from step 2, two 5½" Fabric A squares, two units from step 4, and one 5½" embroidered Fabric B square as shown. Press. Make two and label Rows 4 and 8.

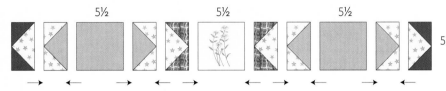

Make 2
Label: Rows 4 and 8

12. Refer to photo on page 98 and quilt layout on page 102. Arrange Rows 1– 11 as shown. Sew rows together. Press.

ADDING THE APPLIQUÉS

Refer to appliqué instructions on page 109. Our instructions are for Quick-Fuse Appliqué, but if you prefer hand appliqué, add ¼"-wide seam allowances.

1. Refer to Quick-Fuse Appliqué on page 109, trace angel patterns onto paper side of fusible web. Use assorted scraps to trace and fuse seven angels, one and one reversed each of Angel #1 and Angel #2, and two and one reversed of Angel #3.

2. Refer to photo on page 98 and layout on page 102. Position and fuse appliqués on quilt as shown. Finish appliqué edges with machine satin stitch or other decorative stitching, as desired.

3. Refer to Embroidery Stitch Guide on page 111. Use two strands of black embroidery floss to make French knots for angels' eyes.

BORDERS

1. Sew 1½" x 42" First Border strips end-to-end to make one continuous 1½"-wide strip. Press. Refer to Adding the Borders on page 110. Measure quilt through center from side to side. Cut two 1½"-wide First Border strips to that measurement. Sew to top and bottom of quilt. Press seams toward border.

2. Measure quilt through center from top to bottom, including borders just added. Cut two 1½"-wide First Border strips to that measurement. Sew to sides of quilt. Press.

3. Refer to steps 1 and 2 to join, measure, trim, and sew 4½"-wide Second Border strips and 1½"-wide Outside Border strips to top, bottom, and sides of quilt. Press seams toward each newly added border strip.

LAYERING & FINISHING

1. Cut backing crosswise into two equal pieces. Sew pieces together to make one 54" x 80" (approximate) backing piece.

2. Arrange and baste backing, batting, and top together, referring to Layering the Quilt on page 110. Hand or machine quilt as desired.

3. Sew 2¾" x 42" binding strips end-to-end to make one continuous 2¾"-wide strip. Refer to Binding the Quilt on page 111 and bind quilt to finish.

Guardian Angel
Crib Quilt Patterns
*Patterns are reversed for use
with Quick-Fuse Appliqué (page 109).*

Tracing Line _____
Tracing Line - - - - - - - - - - - - - - - -
(will be hidden behind other fabrics)

Angel #1
Make 1 and 1 reversed

GUARDIAN ANGEL CRIB QUILT
Finished size: 48" x 68"
Photo: page 98

102

Angel #3
Make 1 and 1 reversed

Angel #2
Make 1 and 1 reversed

Optional
Daisy Embroidery
Pattern

HiT THE ROAD

33" x 36" • Wall Quilt

If you love to "road trip"—or know someone who does—this travel-themed wall quilt is sure to please. Quick-fuse appliqué latches and 3-D handles add detail and whimsy to our three easy-to-piece suitcase blocks. Start packing now: this one goes together so quickly, you'll be "good to go" in no time!

FABRIC REQUIREMENTS & CUTTING INSTRUCTIONS

Read all instructions before beginning and use ¼"-wide seam allowances throughout. Read Cutting Strips and Pieces on page 108 prior to cutting fabrics.

Hit the Road Wall Quilt 33" x 36"	FIRST CUT	
	Number of Strips or Pieces	Dimensions
Fabric A Background ⅜ yard*	2 2 1	11½" x 7½"* 7½" x 3½"* 3½" x 10½"*
Fabric B Large Suitcase ⅓ yard	1	9½" x 24½"*
Fabric C Large Suitcase Trim ⅙ yard	2 2	4½" squares 3" squares
Fabric D Medium Suitcase ¼ yard	1 1	5" x 18½"* 2½" x 18½"*
Fabric E Medium Suitcase Trim ⅛ yard	1	1" x 18½"
Fabric F Small Suitcase ⅓ yard	1	10½" x 8½"*
Fabric G Small Suitcase Trim & Handle ⅛ yard	2	2½" squares
BORDERS		
First Border ⅙ yard	4	1" x 42"
Outside Border ½ yard	4	4" x 42"
Binding ⅜ yard	4	2¾" x 42"

Backing - 1⅛ yards
Batting - 37" x 40" and scraps
Suitcase Latches & Handles - Assorted scraps
Lightweight Fusible Web - Scraps

*Directional fabric is used for all suitcases and Background. Measurement that is listed first runs parallel to selvage.

GETTING STARTED

This quilt includes small, medium, and large suitcase blocks. Each block is a different size, but the block widths are identical so the suitcases "stack" nicely for assembly. We "fussy cut" the background fabric to match the directional print, and used the same fabric—cut on the straight grain—for the binding. The Outside Border is mitered for a clean, tailored look and the suitcase handles are layered with batting to create a dimensional effect.

Refer to Accurate Seam Allowance on page 108. Whenever possible, use the Assembly Line Method on page 108. Press seams in direction of arrows.

SMALL SUITCASE BLOCK

1. Make template using Small Handle Pattern on page 107. Trace handle onto wrong side of fabric scrap and layer with matching fabric, right sides together, over batting. Stitch on drawn lines, leaving ends open for turning. Trim batting close to stitching and cut out handle, leaving ³⁄₁₆"-wide seam allowance. Clip corners and curves, turn right side out, and press.

2. Refer to Quick Corner Triangle Directions on page 108. Sew two 2½" Fabric G squares to one 10½" x 8½" Fabric F piece as shown. Press. Place handle on unit as shown. Baste handle ends to secure. Sew 3½" x 10½" Fabric A piece to unit as shown. Press.

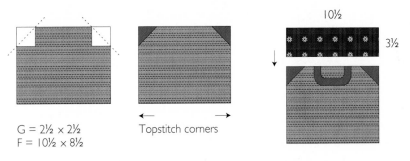

G = 2½ x 2½
F = 10½ x 8½

Topstitch corners

10½

3½

3. Sew unit from step 2 between two 11½" x 7½" Fabric A pieces as shown. Press.

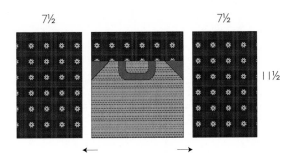

7½   7½

11½

MEDIUM SUITCASE BLOCK

Repeat Small Suitcase Block, step 1 to make Medium Handle using pattern on page 107. Place handle on 5" x 18½" Fabric D strip. Baste handle ends to secure. Sew 1" x 18½" Fabric E strip between 2½" x 18½" Fabric D strip and 5" x 18½" Fabric D strip as shown. Press. Sew unit between two 7½" x 3½" Fabric A pieces as shown. Press.

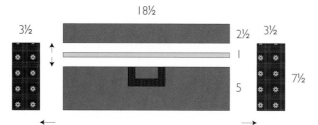

LARGE SUITCASE BLOCK

1. Refer to Quick Corner Triangles on page 108. Sew two 3" Fabric C squares and two 4½" Fabric C squares to 9½" x 24½" Fabric B strip as shown. Press.

C = 3 x 3
C = 4½ x 4½
B = 9½ x 24½

2. Repeat Small Suitcase Block, step 1, to make Large Handle using pattern on page 107. Set handle aside for now.

ADDING THE APPLIQUÉS

1. Refer to Quick-Fuse Appliqué on page 109 and patterns on page 107. Use assorted scraps to trace and cut three of each Small/Large Latch piece, two Medium Latch pieces, and two Large Handle rectangle pieces.

2. Refer to photo on page 104 and layout to position Large Handle on Large Suitcase Block. Cover ends with Large Handle rectangles as shown and fuse rectangles in place to secure. Position and fuse latch appliqués on all Suitcase Blocks. Finish appliqués with machine satin stitch or other decorative stitching as desired.

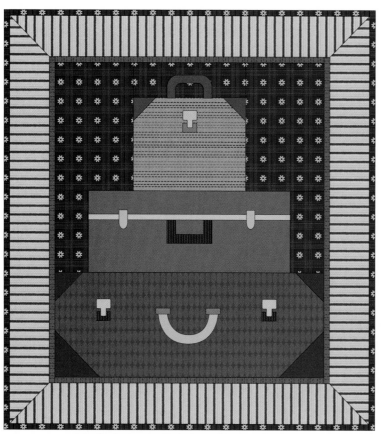

HiT THE ROAD WALL QUiLT
Finished size: 33" x 36"
Photo: page 104

ASSEMBLY

Refer to photo on page 104 and quilt layout. Arrange Small, Medium, and Large Suitcase Blocks in vertical rows. Sew blocks together. Press seams toward Medium Suitcase Block.

BORDERS

1. Refer to Adding the Borders on page 110. Measure quilt through center from side to side. Cut two 1" x 42" First Border strips to that measurement. Sew to top and bottom of quilt. Press seams toward border.

2. Measure quilt through center from top to bottom, including borders just added. Cut two 1"-wide First Border strips to that measurement. Sew to sides of quilt. Press.

3. Refer to Mitered Borders on page 110. Measure, trim, and sew 4" x 42" Outside Border strips to top, bottom, and sides of quilt, mitering corners. Press seams toward Outside Border.

LAYERING & FINISHING

1. Arrange and baste backing, batting, and top together, referring to Layering the Quilt on page 110. Hand or machine quilt as desired.

2. Refer to photo on page 104 and layout. Flip Small Handle up as shown and tack in place with matching-colored thread.

3. Sew 2¾" x 42" binding strips end-to-end to make one continuous 2¾"-wide strip. Refer to Binding the Quilt on page 111 and bind quilt to finish.

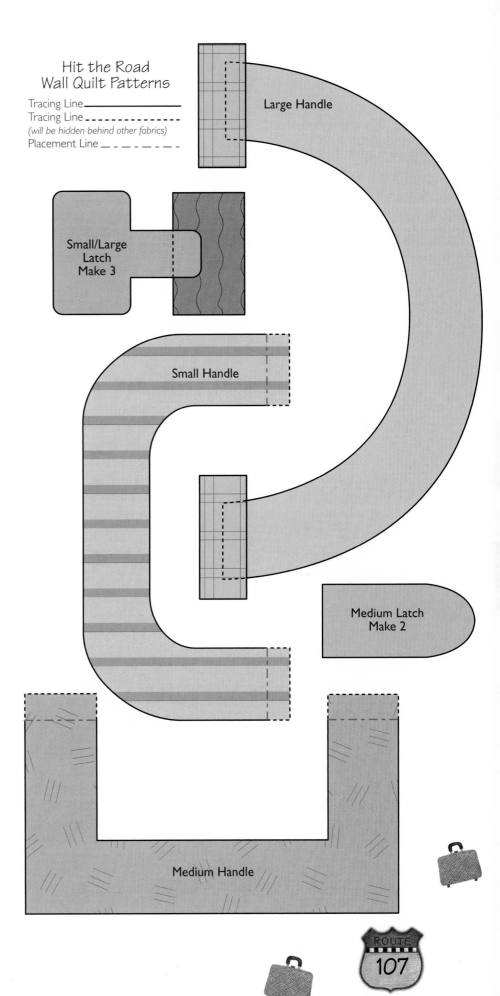

Hit the Road
Wall Quilt Patterns

Tracing Line ————————
Tracing Line - - - - - - - - -
(will be hidden behind other fabrics)
Placement Line — - — - — - —

Large Handle

Small/Large
Latch
Make 3

Small Handle

Medium Latch
Make 2

Medium Handle

GENERAL DiRECTiONS

CUTTING STRIPS & PIECES

We recommend washing cotton fabrics in cold water and pressing before making projects in this book. Using a rotary cutter, see-through ruler, and a cutting mat, cut the strips and pieces for the project. If indicated on the Cutting Chart, some will need to be cut again into smaller strips and pieces. Make second cuts in order shown to maximize use of fabric. The approximate width of the fabric is 42". Measurements for all pieces include ¼"-wide seam allowance unless otherwise indicated. Press in the direction of the arrows.

FUSSY CUT

To make a "fussy cut," carefully position ruler or template over a selected design in fabric. Include seam allowances before cutting desired pieces.

ASSEMBLY LINE METHOD

Whenever possible, use an assembly line method. Position pieces right sides together and line up next to sewing machine. Stitch first unit together, then continue sewing others without breaking threads. When all units are sewn, clip threads to separate. Press in direction of arrows.

ACCURATE SEAM ALLOWANCE

Accurate seam allowances are always important, but especially when the quilt top contains multiple pieced borders with lots of blocks and seams! If each seam is off as little as ¹⁄₁₆", you'll soon find yourself struggling with components that just won't fit.

To ensure seams are a perfect ¼"-wide, try this simple test: Cut three strips of fabric, each exactly 1½" x 12". With right sides together, and long raw edges aligned, sew two strips together, carefully maintaining a ¼" seam. Press. Add the third strip to complete the strip set. Press seams to one side and measure. The finished strip set should measure 3½" x 12". The center strip should measure 1"-wide, the two outside strips 1¼"-wide, and the seam allowances exactly ¼".

If your measurements differ, check to make sure that seams have been pressed flat. If strip set still doesn't "measure up," try stitching a new strip set, adjusting the seam allowance until a perfect ¼"-wide seam is achieved.

Pressing is very important for accurate seam allowances. Press seams using either steam or dry heat with an "up and down" motion. Do not use side-to-side motion as this will distort the unit or block. Set the seam by pressing along the line of stitching, then press seams to one side as indicated by project instructions.

QUICK CORNER TRIANGLES

Quick corner triangles are formed by simply sewing fabric squares to other squares or rectangles. The directions and diagrams with each project illustrate what size pieces to use and where to place squares on the corresponding piece. Follow steps 1–3 below to make quick corner triangle units.

1. With pencil and ruler, draw diagonal line on wrong side of fabric square that will form the triangle. See Diagram A. This will be your sewing line.

A.

sewing line

2. With right sides together, place square on corresponding piece. Matching raw edges, pin in place, and sew ON drawn line. Trim off excess fabric, leaving ¼"-wide seam allowance as shown in Diagram B.

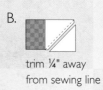

B.

trim ¼" away from sewing line

3. Press seam in direction of arrow as shown in step-by-step project diagram. Measure completed quick corner triangle unit to ensure the greatest accuracy.

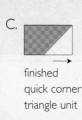

C.

finished quick corner triangle unit

QUICK-FUSE APPLIQUÉ

Quick-fuse appliqué is a method of adhering appliqué pieces to a background with fusible web. For quick and easy results, simply quick-fuse appliqué pieces in place. Use sewable, lightweight fusible web for the projects in this book unless otherwise indicated. Finishing raw edges with stitching is desirable; laundering is not recommended unless edges are finished.

1. With paper side up, lay fusible web over appliqué design. Leaving ½" space between pieces, trace all elements of design. Cut around traced pieces, approximately ¼" outside traced line. See Diagram A.

A.
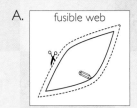
fusible web

2. With paper side up, position and press fusible web to wrong side of selected fabrics. Follow manufacturer's directions for iron temperature and fusing time. Cut out each piece on traced line. See Diagram B.

B.
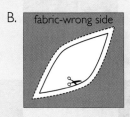
fabric-wrong side

3. Remove paper backing from pieces. A thin film will remain on wrong side of fabric. Position and fuse all pieces of one appliqué design at a time onto background, referring to photos for placement. Fused design will be the reverse of traced pattern.

APPLIQUÉ PRESSING SHEET

An appliqué pressing sheet is very helpful when there are many small elements to apply using a quick-fuse appliqué technique. The pressing sheet allows small items to be bonded together before applying them to the background. The sheet is coated with a special material that prevents fusible web from adhering permanently to the sheet. Follow manufacturer's directions. Remember to let fabric cool completely before lifting it from the appliqué sheet. If not cooled, the fusible web could remain on the sheet instead of on the fabric.

MACHINE APPLIQUÉ

This technique should be used when you are planning to launder quick-fuse projects. Several different stitches can be used: small narrow zigzag stitch, satin stitch, blanket stitch, or another decorative machine stitch. Use an open toe appliqué foot if your machine has one. Use a stabilizer to obtain even stitches and help prevent puckering. Always practice first to check machine settings.

1. Fuse all pieces following Quick-Fuse Appliqué directions.

2. Cut a piece of stabilizer large enough to extend beyond the area to be stitched. Pin to the wrong side of fabric.

3. Select thread to match appliqué.

4. Following the order that appliqués were positioned, stitch along the edges of each section. Anchor beginning and ending stitches by tying off or stitching in place two or three times.

5. Complete all stitching, then remove stabilizer.

HAND APPLIQUÉ

Hand appliqué is easy when you start out with the right supplies. Cotton and machine embroidery thread are easy to work with. Pick a color that matches the appliqué fabric as closely as possible. Use appliqué or silk pins for holding shapes in place and a long, thin needle, such as a sharp, for stitching.

1. Make a template for every shape in the appliqué design. Use a dotted line to show where pieces overlap.

2. Place template on right side of appliqué fabric. Trace around template.

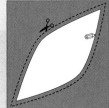

3. Cut out shapes ¼" beyond traced line.

4. Position shapes on background fabric, referring to quilt layout. Pin shapes in place.

5. When layering and stitching appliqué shapes, always work from background to foreground. Where shapes overlap, do not turn under and stitch edges of bottom pieces. Turn and stitch the edges of the piece on top.

6. Use the traced line as your turn-under guide. Entering from the wrong side of the appliqué shape, bring the needle up on the traced line. Using the tip of the needle, turn under the fabric along the traced line. Using blind stitch, stitch along the folded edge to join the appliqué shape to the background fabric. Turn under and stitch about ¼" at a time.

MAKING BIAS STRIPS

1. Refer to Fabric Requirements and Cutting Instructions for the amount of fabric required for the specific bias needed.

2. Remove selvages from the fabric piece and cut into a square. Mark edge with straight pin where selvages were removed as shown. Cut square once diagonally into two equal 45° triangles. (For larger squares, fold square in half diagonally and gently press fold. Open fabric square and cut on fold.)

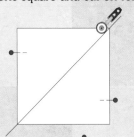

3. Place pinned edges right sides together and stitch along edge with a ¼" seam. Press seam open.

4. Using a ruler and rotary cutter, cut bias strips to width specified in quilt directions.

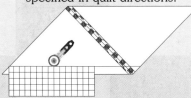

5. Each strip has a diagonal end. To join, place strips perpendicular to each other, right sides together, matching diagonal cut edges and allowing tips of angles to extend approximately ¼" beyond edges. Sew ¼"-wide seams. Continue stitching ends together to make the desired length. Press seams open. Cut strips into recommended lengths according to quilt directions.

ADDING THE BORDERS

1. Measure quilt through the center from side to side. Trim two border strips to this measurement. Sew to top and bottom of quilt. Press seams toward border.

2. Measure quilt through the center from top to bottom, including borders added in step 1. Trim border strips to this measurement. Sew to sides and press. Repeat to add additional borders.

MITERED BORDERS

1. Cut the border strips or strip sets as indicated for quilt.

2. Measure each side of the quilt and mark center with a pin. Fold each border strip crosswise to find its midpoint and mark with a pin. Using the side measurements, measure out from the midpoint and place a pin to show where the edges of the quilt will be.

midpoint

3. Align a border strip to quilt. Pin at midpoints and pin-marked ends first, then along entire side, easing to fit if necessary.

4. Sew border to quilt, stopping and starting ¼" from pin-marked end points. Repeat to sew all four border strips to quilt.

quilt front

5. Fold corner of quilt diagonally, right sides together, matching seams and borders. Place a long ruler along fold line extending across border. Draw a diagonal line across border from fold to edge of border. This is the stitching line. Starting at ¼" mark, stitch on drawn line. Check for squareness, then trim excess. Press seam open.

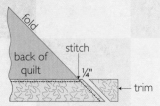

fold

back of quilt

stitch

¼"

trim

LAYERING THE QUILT

1. Cut backing and batting 4" to 8" larger than quilt top.

2. Lay pressed backing on bottom (right side down), batting in middle, and pressed quilt top (right side up) on top. Make sure everything is centered and that backing and batting are flat. Backing and batting will extend beyond quilt top.

3. Begin basting in center and work toward outside edges. Baste vertically and horizontally, forming a 3"–4" grid. Baste or pin completely around edge of quilt top. Quilt as desired. Remove basting.

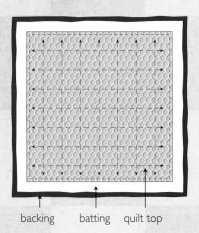

backing   batting   quilt top

BINDING THE QUILT

1. Trim batting and backing to ¼" beyond raw edge of quilt top. This will add fullness to binding.

2. Fold and press binding strips in half lengthwise with wrong sides together.

3. Measure quilt through center from side to side. Cut two binding strips to this measurement. Lay binding strips on top and bottom edges of quilt top with raw edges of binding and quilt top aligned. Sew through all layers, ¼" from quilt edge. Press binding away from quilt top.

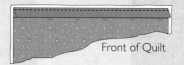
Front of Quilt

4. Measure quilt through center from top to bottom, including binding just added. Cut two binding strips to this measurement and sew to sides through all layers, including binding just added. Press.

5. Folding top and bottom first, fold binding around to back then repeat with sides. Press and pin in position. Hand-stitch binding in place using a blind stitch.

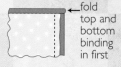
← fold top and bottom binding in first

FINISHING PILLOWS

1. Layer batting between pillow top and lining. Baste. Hand or machine quilt as desired, unless otherwise indicated. Trim batting and lining even with raw edge of pillow top.

2. Narrow hem one long edge of each backing piece by folding under ¼" to wrong side. Press. Fold under ¼" again to wrong side. Press. Stitch along folded edge.

3. With right sides up, lay one backing piece over second piece so hemmed edges overlap, making backing unit the same measurement as the pillow top. Baste backing pieces together at top and bottom where they overlap.

Baste
Baste

4. With right sides together, position and pin pillow top to backing. Using ¼"-wide seam, sew around edges, trim corners, turn right side out, and press.

PILLOW FORMS

Cut two pieces of fabric to finished size of pillow form plus ½". Place right sides together, aligning raw edges. Using ¼"-wide seam, sew around all edges, leaving 4" opening for turning. Trim corners and turn right side out. Stuff to desired fullness with polyester fiberfill and hand-stitch opening closed.

EMBROIDERY STITCH GUIDE

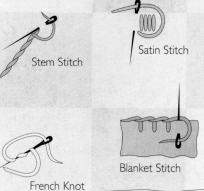
Stem Stitch
Satin Stitch

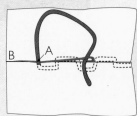
French Knot
Blanket Stitch

Running Stitch

Blind Stitch

COUCHING TECHNIQUE

Couching is a method of attaching a textured yarn, cord, or fiber to fabric for decorative purposes. Use an open-toe embroidery foot or a zigzag presser foot and matching or monofilament thread. Sew with a long zigzag stitch just barely wider than the cord or yarn. Stabilizer on the wrong side of fabric is recommended. Place the yarn, cord, or fiber on right side of fabric and zigzag to attach as shown. A hand-stitch can be used if desired.

Couching

About Debbie Mumm

For nearly twenty years, Debbie Mumm's charming designs and distinctive style have captured the hearts and imaginations of quilters everywhere.

A talented designer and entrepreneur, Debbie got her start in the quilting industry in 1986 with her unique and simple-to-construct quilt patterns. From this beginning, Debbie has led her company to become a multi-faceted enterprise that includes publishing, fabric design, and licensed art divisions.

The author of more than fifty books, Debbie shares her distinctive style with consumers by providing easy-to-follow instructions for quilt and craft projects as well as home decorating tips and inspiration.

At the heart of Debbie's design you will find the warmth and richness of country tradition. Her creative passion is to bring that feeling and those traditional elements together with fresh palettes and modern themes to create the look of today's country.

DESIGNS BY DEBBIE MUMM®
Special thanks to my creative teams:

EDITORIAL & PROJECT DESIGN

Carolyn Ogden: Managing Editor • Georgie Gerl: Quilt and Craft Designer • Carolyn Lowe: Quilt and Craft Designer
Nancy Kirkland: Seamstress/Quilter • Darra Williamson: Technical Writer • Laura M. Reinstatler: Technical Editor
Jackie Saling: Craft Designer • Pam Clarke: Machine Quilter

BOOK DESIGN & PRODUCTION

Mya Brooks: Production Director • Tom Harlow: Graphics Manager • Heather Hughes: Graphic Designer
Gil-Jin Foster: Graphic Designer • Matt Shaffer: Technical Support • Kathy Rickel: Art Studio Assistant

PHOTOGRAPHY

Peter Hassel Photography • Debbie Mumm® Graphics Studio

ART TEAM

Lou McKee: Senior Artist/Designer • Kathy Arbuckle: Artist/Designer • Sandy Ayars: Artist • Heather Butler: Artist • Gil-Jin Foster: Artist

The Debbie Mumm® Sewing Studio exclusively uses Bernina® sewing machines.

©2005 Debbie Mumm

Published by:

Leisure Arts, Inc.
5701 Ranch Drive
Little Rock, AR 72223

Produced by:

Debbie Mumm, Inc.
1116 E. Westview Court
Spokane, WA 99218
(509) 466-3572
Fax (509) 466-6919

www.debbiemumm.com

The information in this publication is presented in good faith, but no warranty is given, nor results guaranteed. Since we have no control over physical conditions surrounding the application of information herein contained, Leisure Arts, Inc. and Debbie Mumm, Inc. disclaim any liability for untoward results.